Football Freaking

Football Freaking

Surreal Sums Behind the Beautiful Game

Gary Rimmer

Icon Books

Published in the UK in 2006 by
Icon Books Ltd, The Old Dairy,
Brook Road, Thriplow,
Cambridge SG8 7RG
email: info@iconbooks.co.uk
www.iconbooks.co.uk

Sold in the UK, Europe, South Africa and Asia
by Faber & Faber Ltd, 3 Queen Square,
London WC1N 3AU
or their agents

Distributed in the UK, Europe, South Africa and Asia
by TBS Ltd, TBS Distribution Centre, Colchester Road,
Frating Green, Colchester CO7 7DW

This edition published in Australia in 2006
by Allen & Unwin Pty Ltd,
PO Box 8500, 83 Alexander Street,
Crows Nest, NSW 2065

Distributed in Canada by
Penguin Books Canada,
90 Eglinton Avenue East, Suite 700,
Toronto, Ontario M4P 2YE

ISBN-10: 1-84046-753-3
ISBN-13: 978-1840467-53-6

Text copyright © 2006 Gary Rimmer

The author has asserted his moral rights.

Typesetting by Hands Fotoset

Printed and bound in the UK by
Creative Print and Design Group

Contents

Zigga-Zagga

Number Freaking is a way of looking at the world through the lens of numbers; twisting numbers to reveal the hidden and surreal mysteries of life. In its black polo-necked jumper, Number Freaking is jazz maths: arithmetic plus extemporisation. In its chunky cardie, meanwhile, Number Freaking is doodling with numbers, in your head, just for fun – as revealed in *Number Freaking: The Surreal Sums Behind Everyday Life* (2006).

But now, Number Freaking has hung its woollies on its coat hook, slipped into its number 9 shirt and run onto the pitch as Football Freaking – a way of twisting numbers to reveal the hidden and surreal mysteries of the people's ballet.

Some might say *Football Freaking* is just advanced stats and not much about the football at all. But *Football Freaking* will tell you things about the game you never knew before. From the World Cup to the FA Cup, from the foundation of the modern game in 1863 right up until now in 2006, *Football Freaking* will reveal things you didn't know you didn't know.

You may think you know who ate the pies, but do you know how much beef went into them? Or what Rio Ferdinand could earn cleaning his teeth? Or what Wayne Rooney might be worth in kippers? Or how many men will die if England lose the World Cup in Germany? Only *Football Freaking* can tell.

Football Freaking is neither a work of reference nor a definitive source. It's not a betting system and the information contained herein should not be used as a basis for investment decisions. Why? Because *Football Freaking* isn't about being right; it's for fun. Be prepared to guesstimate, speculate and extrapolate. All you need to join in is a calculator – and maybe a visit later to www.footballfreaking.co.uk.

This isn't to say *Football Freaking* is without opinions. As an invaluable accompaniment to your World Cup pleasure 2006, *Football Freaking* is proud to offer a comprehensive copper-bottomed forecast of the result to every single game in this summer's forthcoming German World Cup. Why not see how well we got on? However, as every forecast was made before a ball had been kicked and the World Cup won't actually start until after this book hits the shops, it would probably be unwise to use these forecasts as a gambling aid.

So what else do you need to know? That in this book £1 is fixed at US $1.7712 or €1.4782 (so €1 = US $1.1982 = £0.6765). Single years are assumed to contain 365 days, but over longer periods are calculated at 365.25 days each. Other conversion values such as 1 mile = 1.6093 kilometre and 1 kilogram = 2.205 pounds are standard international conventions. Whether answers are rounded up or down depends on the question.

Moving on, thanks are due to the editing and marketing teams at Icon, both old and new. And to everyone whose feelings were hurt, toes trodden upon, or integrity called into question in the production of this book, you get a sorry too.

And finally, just how hidden are the numbers in this book? Well, how about this? The word *soccer* is a corruption of the word *socca*, itself an abbreviation of *association football*. The use of the word *socca* can be traced back to 1889 and the word *soccer* to 1895 ...

And so in this book, the word *football* physically occupies about 9 square millimetres more paper than the word *soccer*. Assume this is a worldwide average. Therefore, every million times the word football is used in print instead of the word soccer, it consumes 720 grams more paper (at 80 grams per square metre) and the wood it takes to make. Now think how many millions – even billions – of times the word football must be printed instead of the word soccer every year, and what can we conclude? Soccer is more eco-friendly than football because soccer literally conserves more trees. QED.

About The Author

Before he was stripped of his rank and dishonourably discharged, Gary Rimmer was a mid-field general. He never played for Brazil.

Squad Size

Here are the sizes of the playing squads of every team in the English Premiership.

		Total squad			Total squad
1	Chelsea	22	11	Charlton Athletic	22
2	Liverpool	20	12	Blackburn Rovers	22
3	Manchester United	20	13	Middlesbrough	26
4	Tottenham Hotspur	23	14	Aston Villa	24
5	Bolton Wanderers	22	15	Everton	20
6	Arsenal	20	16	Fulham	19
7	Wigan Athletic	20	17	West Bromwich Albion	23
8	Manchester City	22	18	Birmingham City	23
9	West Ham United	18	19	Portsmouth	24
10	Newcastle United	23	20	Sunderland	24

i. What is the average playing squad size in the Premiership?

a) 23.15
b) 21.85
c) 20.55

(Nowhere in the book of rules does it say you can't field 0.85 of a player.)

Answer: i) b

The Dutch international squad has 33 players.

Man Size

There are 23 players in the England playing squad; the England squad is bigger than the average Premiership squad.

The 2002 World Cup opened in Seoul on Friday, 31 May 2002.

This is the squad sent by England.

Player	Height	Player	Height	Player	Height
David Seaman	6' 3"	Robbie Fowler	5' 11"	Teddy Sheringham	6' 1"
Danny Mills	5' 11"	Michael Owen	5' 8"	Owen Hargreaves	5' 11"
Ashley Cole	5' 9"	Emile Heskey	6' 2"	Joe Cole	5' 9"
Trevor Sinclair	5' 10"	Wes Brown	6' 1"	Darius Vassell	5' 7"
Rio Ferdinand	6' 2"	Nigel Martyn	6' 1"	Nicky Butt	5' 10"
Sol Campbell	6' 2"	Wayne Bridge	5' 10"	David James	6' 5"
David Beckham	5' 11"	Martin Keown	6'1"	Kieron Dyer	5' 7"
Paul Scholes	5' 7"	Gareth Southgate	6' 0"		

i. How tall was this England squad on average?

a) 6' 3"
b) 6' 1½"
c) 5' 11¼"

Back in the football mists of 2002 the England goal keeping squad for the 2002 World Cup had an average height of 6' 3", the defence 6' 0", the midfield 5' 9¼" and the forwards 5' 11¼".

How will this ultimately compare with 2006? Send your answers to www.footballfreaking.co.uk.

Answer: i) c

Jan Koller the Czech Republic striker is 6' 7½" tall.

Stronger

This is the England squad that turned out for a friendly against Argentina in Geneva in the months preceding the 2006 World Cup.

Starters	Height	Fielded subs	Height	Unfielded subs	Height
Paul Robinson	6' 3"	Peter Crouch	6' 7"	Robert Green	6' 2"
Luke Young	5' 11"	Paul Konchesky	5' 10"	David James	6' 5"
Rio Ferdinand	6' 2"	Joe Cole	5' 9"	Phil Neville	5' 11"
John Terry	6' 2"			Sol Campbell	6' 2"
Wayne Bridge	5' 10"			Michael Carrick	6' 0"
David Beckham	5' 11"			Jermaine Jenas	5' 11"
Ledley King	6' 2"			Shaun Wright-Phillips	5' 6"
Frank Lampard	6' 0"			Alan Smith	5' 8"
Steven Gerrard	6' 1"			Jermain Defoe	5' 7"
Wayne Rooney	5' 10"				
Michael Owen	5' 8"				

i. How tall are this England squad on average?

a) 5' 11¾"
b) 5' 10½"
c) 6' 2"

So bigger than the last lot then ... just. (By about a centimetre in fact.)

Answer: i) a

Norwegian forward Tor Hogne Aaroy is 6' 8¼" tall.

Cobblers

Football: it's about balls and it's about foots.

The science of anthropometry measures your feet as 15.2% of your height. A man's UK shoe size is roughly 3 times his foot length in inches, minus 22. Accordingly, Nwankwo Kanu – the Nigeria and West Bromwich Albion striker – who is 6′ 5″, should have feet 11.7″ long and be shoe size 13. But Nwankwo was once identified in the *International Herald Tribune* as the man with the biggest feet in soccer. Now, whether this is true is a matter between the man and his cobbler. But size 13 – the biggest feet in football? I think not ...

Peter Crouch of Liverpool and England is reportedly 6′ 7″ tall.

i. How big, according to anthropometry, should his feet be?

a) 12″
b) 13″
c) 17″

ii. And what size shoe does Football Freaking suggest that he takes?

a) 13
b) 14
c) 16

So if you happen to meet him you can ask him if it's true ...

Answers: i) a ii) b

Shin protectors (made from old cricket pads) were first introduced in 1874.

Younger

It isn't just boot size that counts. The 2002 World Cup opened in Seoul on Friday, 31 May 2002. This is the squad sent by England and their dates of birth and their ages in days at the opening.

Player	Date of birth	Days	Player	Date of birth	Days
David Seaman	19.09.63	14,134	Nigel Martyn	11.08.66	13,077
Danny Mills	18.05.77	9,144	Wayne Bridge	05.08.80	7,969
Ashley Cole	20.12.80	7,832	Martin Keown	24.07.66	13,095
Trevor Sinclair	02.03.73	10,682	Gareth Southgate	03.09.70	11,593
Rio Ferdinand	07.11.78	8,606	Teddy Sheringham	02.04.66	13,208
Sol Campbell	18.09.74	10,117	Owen Hargreaves	20.01.81	7,801
David Beckham	02.05.75	9,891	Joe Cole	08.11.81	7,509
Paul Scholes	16.11.74	10,058	Darius Vassell	13.06.80	8,022
Robbie Fowler	09.04.75	9,914	Nicky Butt	21.01.75	9,992
Michael Owen	14.12.79	8,204	David James	08.01.70	11,831
Emile Heskey	11.01.78	8,906	Kieron Dyer	29.12.78	8,554
Wes Brown	13.10.79	8,266			

Now technically you can't have an average birthday – unless you're Football Freaking.

i. What was the average age of the England squad picked for the 2002 World Cup on the day the finals started?

a) 22 years 4 months 8 days
b) 27 years 2 months 7 days
c) 31 years 8 months 15 days

- *This gives an average birthday of 24 March 1975.*

Answers: i) b

The global median age is currently 27 years 7 months.

This is the England squad that turned out for a friendly against Argentina in the months preceding the 2006 World Cup.

Starters	Date of birth	Days	Fielded subs	Date of birth	Days
Paul Robinson	15.10.79	9,734	Peter Crouch	01.01.81	9,290
Luke Young	19.07.79	9,822	Paul Konchesky	15.05.81	9,156
Rio Ferdinand	07.11.78	10,076	Joe Cole	08.11.81	8,979
John Terry	07.12.80	9,315			
Wayne Bridge	05.08.80	9,439	Unfielded subs	Date of birth	Days
David Beckham	02.05.75	11,361	Robert Green	18/01/80	9,639
Ledley King	10.12.80	9,312	David James	08.01.70	13,301
Frank Lampard	21.06.78	10,215	Phil Neville	21.01.77	10,731
Steven Gerrard	30.05.80	9,506	Sol Campbell	18.09.74	11,587
Wayne Rooney	24.10.85	7,533	Michael Carrick	28.07.81	9,082
Michael Owen	14.12.79	9,674	Jermaine Jenas	18.02.83	8,512
			Shaun Wright-Phillips	25.10.81	8,993
			Alan Smith	20.10.80	9,363
			Jermain Defoe	07.10.82	8,646

ii. What will be the average age of this squad on 9 June, the first day of World Cup 2006?

a) 24 years 1 month 28 days
b) 26 years 6 months 28 days
c) 33 years 9 months 15 days

- *This gives an average birthday of 11 November 1979.*

So this squad is taller than the 2002 England team and younger too. Would you make the cut?

You can calculate their star signs for yourself.

Answer: ii) b

In 1930, Yugoslavia's team vs. Brazil was the youngest ever to play in the World Cup: average age 21 years 258 days.

Odds Off

Every year, 600 16-year-old boys are recruited into England's professional game.

There are 333,723 boys born in the UK every year. So assume this is the number of 16-year-olds too.

> **i. So one in how many of these boys will be recruited into England's professional game at the age of 16?**
>
> a) 557
> b) 1,206
> c) 304

And so to scrape together a team of 11 boys good enough for the professional game, you'd have to look at 6,108 others. No wonder they call them football scouts.

Age Before Beauty

The record for the youngest player ever to run out in the English Premiership currently belongs to Aaron Lennon of Leeds United, who played against Tottenham in August 2003 at the age of 16 years 129 days. The record for the youngest player to play in the league, meanwhile, has stood for over 50 years. It's held jointly by two men, Albert Geldard and Ken Roberts, who both made their debuts at the age of 15 years 158 days ...

So let's assume no Premiership player will ever be younger than 15.

Answer: i) a

There are 39 FA-accredited football academies in England.

Meanwhile, the oldest player ever to appear in the Premiership was goalie John Burridge, who turned out for Manchester City against QPR in 1995 at the age of 43 years 5 months. So let's assume that no Premiership player will ever be older than 44.

- *The oldest player ever to turn out in the old first division was Sir Stanley Matthews for Stoke City against Fulham in 1965, aged 50 years 5 days.*

There are 12,404,315 men in the UK aged 15–44.

Now, for the sake of argument, assume there are no 'foreign' players in the English Premiership (as if – but bear with us), and that these 12,404,315 men are the pool for players who might occupy Premiership starting places in any given week.

There are 220 starting places available in the Premiership (11 starts for 20 teams).

---

i. So how many men theoretically compete for each starting place every week?

a) 30,222
b) 56,383
c) 87,743

In other words, everything being equal, the odds on a British man aged 15–44 picked at random donning a Premiership shirt and walking out onto the pitch to start a game is 56,383 to 1.

The absolutely oldest UK league appearance ever was by a former Everton centre-half turned club manager named Neil McBain. He appeared as an emergency goalkeeper in March 1947 at the age of 52 years 4 months. His

---

Answer: i) b

In 1998, the German team facing Iran was the oldest ever to play in the World Cup, with an average age of 31 years 345 days.

team, New Brighton, lost the game 3:0 to Hartlepool United. So obviously, Mr McBain didn't so much play as an emergency goalkeeper, but as a rubbish goalkeeper.

By the by, your chance of winning the jackpot on the lottery is reported to be about 14 million to 1. (About the same, apparently, as the odds you'll die in a fatal accident involving a fridge.) 14 million divided by 56,383 is about 250 (248.3 to be more exact).

So again, everything being equal, in any one week a man aged 15–44 has 250 times more chance of starting a game as a Premiership footballer than he has of winning a lottery jackpot. But of course, if ever he does start a game as a Premiership footballer, he's already won a lottery jackpot ...

Richer

The richest player in England is reputed to be David Beckham, said to earn (including endorsements) £17 million a year.

If the England team wins the 2006 World Cup, they've been promised a £300,000 bonus each.

i. How long does it take David Beckham to earn £300,000 usually?

a) 12.21 days
b) 3.44 days
c) 6.44 days

The average salary for men in work in the UK is currently £30,948 for a 365-day year.

Answer: i) c

Zidane cost Real £47 million, Ronaldo €47 million: at this book's exchange rate a Ronaldo is 0.6765 Zidanes.

ii. How much does the average man in the UK earn in 6.44 days?

a) £433.89
b) £673.22
c) £546.04

Which is about the same as a useful Christmas bonus.

Premiership players reputedly earn an average basic salary of £676,000 a year plus bonuses.

Mobile Operator

About 18 million extra text messages were sent in the UK on the day in November 2003 that England beat Australia in the Rugby World Cup Final.

Assume a causal link between this match result and this increase in text traffic. Assume the result of any England game in the soccer World Cup will generate as many extra text messages as the result of an English appearance at a Rugby World Cup Final.

i. At £0.30 a call, how much additional income could the results from each of England's matches at the 2006 World Cup produce for mobile phone operators in the UK?

a) £540,000
b) £15.4 million
c) £5.4 million

Answers: ii) c i) c

64 World Cup finals matches – with 22 players and 3 officials per game – equals 3,200 sweaty socks.

- *Total cost of the £300,000 bonus for the 23 squad members after an overall England win: £6.9 million*

Assume England go all the way and play 7 matches – 3 at the groups stage, 1 in the second round, 1 quarter-final, 1 semi-final and then either the 3rd place play-off or the Final itself – and that the results from each match generate 18 million extra text messages each.

> **ii. At £0.30 a call, how much additional income could England's 7 match results at the 2006 World Cup produce in total for mobile phone operators in the UK?**
>
> a) £3.78 million
> b) £37.8 million
> c) £378,000

- *Most recent transfer fees of Wayne Rooney and Michael Owen combined: £37 million*
- *If this texting phenomenon were replicated worldwide it would yield: £345.6 million*

All Change Is Good

The G-14 European Football Clubs Grouping ...

Real Madrid CF	FC Internazionale Milano	Futebol Clube do Porto	AC Milan
Olympique Lyonnais	Liverpool FC	Juventus FC	AFC Ajax
FC Barcelona	Manchester United FC	Borussia Dortmund	Arsenal FC
Olympique de Marseille	Paris Saint-Germain	Bayer 04 Leverkusen	Valencia CF
FC Bayern München	PSV		

Answer: ii) b

A total of 26 billion texts were sent in the UK in 2004.

... think they should run international club competitions in which their member clubs are involved. It's not an idea the current bosses of international football are wild about. But it's hard to imagine that G-14 won't eventually get their way.

If they haven't started already the big clubs are globalising now. The Glazer family has been vilified for acquiring Manchester United (MU). Their crime was seeing what football might become before anyone else (except maybe Roman Abramovitch). Their punishment may be that it's the second mouse that gets the cheese.

The buzz phrase in football's corridors of power is global brand extension: capitalising on a club's name overseas. For example, MU have embarked on a programme to open 100 MU-themed restaurants in Asia (many of them in China), have signed teenage Chinese striker Dong Fangzhou from Dalian Shide, have toured Japan and China (where they beat Beijing Hyundai 3:0 in the Budweiser Manchester United Beijing Cup in front of a half-empty stadium) and now have a Chinese website. You know what they say, if it looks like a plan, smells like a plan and tastes like a plan ...

China accounts for approximately 20% of the world's population.

> **i. If MU opens, say, 80 restaurants in China, how many must they open pro-rata worldwide so we can all enjoy MU food?**
>
> a) 40
> b) 400
> c) 4,000

We may not see a World Cup like 2006 again. By 2010, will top players be sporting divas booked for the weekend by the highest paying stadium? We'll know in South Africa. We may look back on 2006 and think how utterly quaint and parochial football used to be ...

Answer: i) b

Real Madrid is reported to have earned £422,000 in shirt sales on the day David Beckham transferred in.

And the Winner is Brazil

The publication date of this book, 1 June 2006, was a full week before the 2006 World Cup kicked off in Munich. However, *Football Freaking* can confidently predict the World Cup will be won by Brazil, who will beat Argentina in Berlin. England (perhaps you'll be pleased to hear) will take 3rd place.

A full list of equally confident predictions as to the outcome of every match in the World Cup – from the opening day when Germany will beat Costa Rica and Poland will beat Ecuador, via the second round, quarters, semis and the explosive Final in Berlin – are at the back of this book.

To 'forecast' these results, *Football Freaking* weighs together five things. First, historic match results: for example, England have played and beaten their first opponent Paraguay twice with an aggregate score of 7:0. Second, FIFA world rankings: at the time of writing England are ranked 9 and Paraguay 30. Both facts support a compelling case for an England win. But when the data is less clear or when the data is non-existent (for example, England have never actually played Trinidad and Tobago), forecasts are based on country populations and per capita GDPs.

Players representing the hopes of around a fifth of the world's population are expected in Germany.

Population is a measure of the pool of available talent; since bigger countries are more likely to produce protégés, it should predict the victor. Hence Trinidad and Tobago is tiny so England will beat them ... But it also begs the question: why then do the Swedes keep beating England? Hold that thought.

Per capita GDP is an economist's measure of average wealth and is a relative measure of access to physical fitness, training and infrastructure. It means Trinidad and Tobago is poor so England will beat them ... Well they should do, anyway.

Here is a list of FIFA rankings, populations and per capita GDPs.

	FIFA rank	Population	Per capita GDP €	Single airfare to Munich €
Group A				
Germany	16	82,431,390	23,950	------
Costa Rica	21	4,016,173	8,010	1,375.9
Poland	23	38,557,984	10,015	578.4
Ecuador	37	13,363,593	3,090	1,915.5
Group B				
England	9	50,598,940	24,700	176.5
Paraguay	30	6,347,884	4,005	701.9
Trinidad and Tobago	51	1,088,644	9,235	2,454.2
Sweden	14	9,001,774	23,700	884.3
Group C				
Argentina	4	39,537,943	10,350	822.3
Côte d'Ivoire	41	17,298,040	1,250	1,774.7
Serbia and Montenegro	47	10,829,175	2,000	733.2
Netherlands	3	16,407,491	9,515	730.1
Group D				
Mexico	7	106,202,903	8,010	1,515.9
Iran	19	68,017,860	6,425	394.5
Angola	62	11,827,315	1,750	1,769.0
Portugal	10	10,566,212	14,940	391.1
Group E				
Italy	12	58,103,033	23,120	713.1
Ghana	50	21,946,247	1,900	1,927.4
United States	8	295,734,134	33,450	2,015.3
Czech Republic	2	10,241,138	14,780	584.4

Continued	FIFA rank	Population	Per capita GDP €	Single airfare to Munich €
Group F				
Brazil	1	186,112,794	6,760	1,286.8
Croatia	20	4,495,904	9,350	974.7
Australia	49	20,090,437	27,000	809.5
Japan	15	127,417,244	24,500	2,913.1
Group G				
France	5	60,656,178	23,950	574.0
Switzerland	36	7,489,370	29,730	334.5
South Korea	29	48,640,671	16,025	3,719.0
Togo	56	5,399,991	1,335	1,795.9
Group H				
Spain	6	40,341,462	20,490	121.3
Ukraine	40	46,996,765	5,250	878.5
Tunisia	28	10,074,951	5,925	325.5
Saudi Arabia	32	26,417,599	10,015	1,373.7

This list also shows single airfares from the main air hub in each country to Munich Franz Josef Strauss Airport. For the USA, this was taken to be from O'Hare Airport in Chicago (the home of the US Soccer Federation).

A playing squad is 23 players. In the case of England, the National Team Staff, the coaches, medics and kit managers etc., number at least 12 people (as on tour in the USA in 2005). It can be more – Sweden's 2005 UEFA Women's Championship support team numbered 19 people. We'll assume the average size of a national support staff for a team in the World Cup is 15 ... so this will take the total number of air passengers a side to 38.

The single airfare from Sydney to Munich, for example, is currently €809.50. For a group of 38, that's over €30,761 each way. However, since the average Aussie has a per capita GDP of €27,000, it'll only take the annual output of

1.14 (1¹/₇) Australians to drum up the cash. For England, it'll be even less. London to Munich is only €176.50 single, or €6,707 for a squad of 38. An average Brit worker generates this much output in about 14 weeks.

Compare this with the example of Côte d'Ivoire. The single airfare from Abidjan to Munich is currently €1,774.70 per head, and per capita annual GDP is only €1,250.

> **i. In Côte d'Ivoire, how many average workers' monthly outputs will it take to send 38 people, return, to Munich?**
>
> a) 687
> b) 1,296
> c) 2,314

Relatively, it will cost Côte d'Ivoire some 200 times more than it will the UK to attend the World Cup in airfares alone.

It will take the entire annual output of over 7 average Brazilians to fly a squad of 38 Brazilian players, coaches, medics and officials to Munich – though presumably they think it's worth it.

Is There a Single Room Surcharge?

It's the subject of urban myth that after scoring a goal in the 1966 World Cup Final, Jack Charlton had to sleep on a friend's floor in Stoke Newington because he had nowhere else to stay.

At the time of writing, the Munich Hilton room rate is €86 a night. We'll assume it's an appropriate guide price for a hotel room in Germany (so in Berlin, Hamburg, Gelsenkirshen, Leipzig, etc. as well) of a standard good enough to accommodate an international team (and their support staff). So

---

Answer: i) b

The first 'proper' football match recorded in Brazil was played on 19 June 1894.

38 people in an international squad means a nightly bill (leaving aside drinks from the mini-bar, dry cleaning, phone calls home, an ice cream for the ball boy, whatever) of €3,268 for every night a team stays in the competition.

Taking the example of Côte d'Ivoire again, they'll need to be in Germany for the opening game on 9 June (so will need to be in the country no later than the night of 8 June). They have their last group match on 21 June – so they won't be able to leave Germany until at least 22 June (a stay of 14 nights, minimum).

> **i. How much for 14 nights of hotel accommodation (without extras) for 38 people?**
>
> a) €45,752
> b) €15,221
> c) €75,599

So far then we know that just getting the Côte d'Ivoire squad to Germany on a plane and then sticking them in a hotel for 2 weeks during the group stage (without worrying about feeding them or transporting them from match to match) will cost €113,191. This is the entire fortnightly gross domestic product of 2,354 other Côte d'Ivoirians; 2,354 other Côte d'Ivoirians who won't be lounging around eating cake and sipping fizzy drinks in fancy German hotels on a 14-night break in the Rhineland ... 2,354 Côte d'Ivoirians who will therefore be expecting an awful lot from their boys.

Hotel accommodation isn't an issue for the biggest teams: Castrop-Rauxel, formerly a small coal-mining town near Dortmund, with a population of just 80,000, has agreed to pay Brazil €500,000 to stay at its deluxe hotel during the World Cup. England, meanwhile, are staying in Baden-Baden. Germany will be staying in Berlin, Sweden will be in Bremen, Argentina in Herzogenaurach, and the Netherlands in Hinterzarten. The USA will stay in Hamburg.

Answer: i) a

At the last count, 806,500 hotel rooms were available in Germany, at an average price of €83 a night each.

So the One Who Pays Most Airfare Most Wants to Win?

The CIA identifies 271 nations, dependent areas, and other administrative divisions. The United Nations, as of 2005, has 191 member states, including virtually all internationally recognised independent nations. FIFA counts 207 member countries. More countries belong to FIFA than the UN.

Appearing at the World Cup does marvellous things for a nation's sense of prestige and morale. When Togo qualified for the 2006 World Cup finals, President Faure Gnassingbe declared a national holiday and the team were feted in the national stadium in Lome by a crowd of over 30,000 ...

But after Pierre Wome missed a free kick that cost Cameroon their place at the same tournament, furious fans looted his home, wrecked his Mercedes and turned over his girlfriend's hair salon; and he had to be smuggled out of the country. When the Côte d'Ivoirian football team lost in the 2000 Cup of Nations, they were punished with 3 days of hard military training. None of which is as unlucky as defender Andres Escobar, who was shot dead for scoring an own goal in a match against the USA (and knocking Colombia out early from USA 1994).

Because the fifth variable *Football Freaking* recognises must be factored in when forecasting the outcome of World Cup matches is determination, grit, guts, resolve, the urge to win against the odds, faith, belief, the 'it's-not-the-dog-in-the-fight-it's-the-fight-in-the-dog' factor: the hunger. (That's why Trinidad and Tobago, although tiny, want to beat England so badly they just might ... and why Sweden keep beating England.)

But how do we measure this? Since Football Freaking is only for fun, we can create any theory we like. So we'll assume, for the sake of this book, and please remember this is being written in advance, that the relative determin-ation of any given team to win at the 2006 World Cup shall be determined by the relative expense of their airfares to Germany. Sure, on the face of it, it's a scale that's both arbitrary and ridiculous, but it's an index that ranks countries relative to their wealth and population. And on the up side, it means nobody can accuse Football Freaking of being a serious betting system. (Feel free to dismiss it as nonsense and calculate your own index.)

This table shows the number of average locals from each country who need to work for a year to pay 38 people's airfare to Munich.

Côte d'Ivoire	53.95	Costa Rica	6.53	Czech Republic	1.50
Togo	51.12	Ukraine	6.36	Sweden	1.42
Ghana	38.55	Saudi Arabia	5.21	Italy	1.17
Ecuador	23.56	Japan	4.52	Australia	1.14
Serbia and Montenegro	13.93	Croatia	3.96	Portugal	0.99
Angola	38.41	Argentina	3.02	France	0.91
Trinidad and Tobago	10.10	Netherlands	2.92	Switzerland	0.48
South Korea	8.82	Iran	2.33	England	0.27
Brazil	7.23	United States	2.29	Spain	0.22
Mexico	7.19	Poland	2.19	Germany	----
Paraguay	6.66	Tunisia	2.09		

The higher this number (we'll call it their Football Freaking Factor or 3F), the greater the cost we'll assume to that country. And that, we'll infer, is a measure of just how much, relatively, they want to win ...

How could a Football Freaker use this table? Well, Trinidad and Tobago have been allocated a 'score' of 10.1 and England a 'score' of 0.27. The ratio of these two (10.1 divided by 0.27) is roughly 37 – which *Football Freaking* will take to indicate that Trinidad and Tobago are roughly 37 times hungrier to win than England. Not that it'll do them any good ...

i. Côte d'Ivoire's 3F is 53.95 and Serbia and Montenegro's is 13.93. Côte d'Ivoire feel roughly how many times more determined?

a) 6.2
b) 9.4
c) 3.9

Put another way, according to *Football Freaking*, when Côte d'Ivoire play Serbia and Montenegro on 21 June, while they won't have made it through to the second round, they're going to win 2:1.

Old Men's Game

A man's life expectancy in the Côte d'Ivoire is slightly less than 46 years 7½ months. So the odds are goalie John Burridge – the oldest man, you will remember, ever to play in the English Premiership – the man who turned out for Manchester City at the age of 43 years 5 months in 1995 – probably wouldn't still be alive in Côte d'Ivoire, let alone playing a first-class game ...

The median age in the Côte d'Ivoire (the age exactly half the population are younger than) is less than 19 years 5 months. Therefore, half of the men in Côte d'Ivoire are 7 years younger than the England squad (previously discussed) selected to play Argentina. To Côte d'Ivorian eyes, England is a team of old men.

Answer: i) c
Côte d'Ivoire didn't make its international debut until April 1960, when it beat Benin 3:2.

Here is a list of noteworthy Côte d'Ivoirian players, their dates of birth, and how many days each will have been alive at the start of the 2006 World Cup.

Player	Date of birth	Days	Player	Date of birth	Days
Ibrahima Bakayoko	31.12.76	10,752	Emmanuel Eboué	14.01.83	8,547
Didier Drogba	11.03.78	10,080	Bakary Koné	17.09.81	9,031
Arouna Koné	11.11.83	8,246	Aruna Dindane	26.11.80	9,326
Yaya Touré	13.05.83	8,428	Bonaventure Kalou	12.01.78	10,375
Kolo Touré	19.03.81	9,213			

i. What will be the average age of these players on 9 June 2006?

a) 25 years 6 months 20 days
b) 22 years 4 months 20 days
c) 19 years 3 months 18 days

- *The average birthday of these men falls on: 19 November 1980*

Half of the men in Côte d'Ivoire are therefore over 6 years younger than Côte d'Ivoire's footballing best – so to Côte d'Ivorians, their team is made up of old men too. Football must seem a game in which you aim to succeed very much in the second half of your life – at an age equivalent in England to around, say, 43 ...

In England, men have a median age of close to 37 years 11 months. Consequently, more men in England see the England team as younger than themselves rather than older. In Côte d'Ivoire, however, the men in the national

Answer: i) a

Construction on Cidadella, Angola's national football stadium, began in 1977. It's still unfinished.

team are conspicuously the nation's seniors; an inspiration as to what you might become rather than a testimony to what you might have been.

In a place like Cote d'Ivoire, football is an escape from grim realities and cheerless lives. As Côte d'Ivoire emerges from a brutal civil war, the talk is of free elections in October 2006 ... maybe. A good – or bad – showing by Côte d'Ivoire's Elephants in the World Cup could have a demonstrable impact. Rather more of a responsibility than Becks and the England boys have ever had to carry.

As Bill Shankly put it: 'Some people believe football is a matter of life and death. I'm very disappointed with that attitude. I can assure you it is much, much more important than that.'

Man Power

Those nice people from G-14 also want national football associations to field the tab on salaries due under club contracts, while national team players are on national duty. Fine and dandy if you're Robert Huth and the national association is Germany, but what if you're the Côte d'Ivoire and have to pay the club salary due to Didier Drogba?

We don't know exactly what these men earn, but we do know a Chelsea player (like Robert Huth or Didier Drogba) can earn a weekly wage between £40,000 and £100,000 (about €60,000 and €150,000). So we'll assume they both earn 'only' £40,000 a week. We also know the 2006 World Cup lasts 30 days and the per capita GDP in Germany, at the time of writing, is €23,950 (about £16,202) and in Côte d'Ivoire it's €1,250 (about £846).

The other thing we know, at the time of writing, is that Chelsea aren't represented by G-14. This Football Freak is therefore entirely fictional.

i. How many man-years of average Côte d'Ivoirian productivity would it take to pay Didier Drogba his Chelsea salary during a month at the World Cup.

a) 355.8
b) 202.6
c) 111.1

Or put another way, it takes a month's work by 2,431 Côte d'Ivoirians to generate a month of Didier's salary.

ii. How many man-years of average German productivity would it take to pay Robert Huth his Chelsea salary during a month at the World Cup.

a) 17.1
b) 13.5
c) 10.6

So, what it takes 2,431 Côte d'Ivorian's to do for Didier it takes only 127 Germans to do for Robert; 19 Côte d'Ivorian's to do what 1 German can.

(And remember these numbers are based on a weekly wage of 'only' £40,000 a week. Feel free to recalculate these numbers for a salary of £100,000 a week.)

Rich Men's Playthings

So suddenly you're a Russian billionaire. Or American. And you have a wallet stuffed with cash and a yen to buy yourself a team in the Premiership ... Hell you're a Russian or American billionaire with a yen to start your own team and the juice to steamroller it through the FA. So, why not buy the best you can? Assume they're all for sale. You decide to buy yourself the England squad – or at least the England squad selected for the match against Argentina in November 2005 ...

So do you believe Steven Gerrard is worth the £32 million he reputedly walked away from to stay at Anfield? Do you believe Ledley King is worth £12 million? Or £20 million? Is £3 million a fair price for Robert Green? And is John Terry – if he was for sale – worth the £50 million plus that Jose Mourinho reportedly thinks he is? We can't know; none of these players has a transfer history to compare with.

These, however, are the most recent transfer fees paid, that can be found in the public record, for players in an England squad fielded against Argentina in November 2005.

Player	Transfer fee (£ million)	Player	Transfer fee (£ million)
Paul Robinson	1.5	Peter Crouch	7
Luke Young	4	Paul Konchesky	1.5
Rio Ferdinand	29.1	Joe Cole	6.6
Wayne Bridge	7	Phil Neville	3.5
David Beckham	17.25	Jermaine Jenas	7
Frank Lampard	11	Shaun Wright-Phillips	21
Wayne Rooney	20	Alan Smith	6
Michael Owen	17	Jermain Defoe	6

i. Based on these figures, what is the combined transfer value of these England players?

a) £165.5 million
b) £234.7 million
c) £93.8 million

- *Price paid by Roman Abramovich for control of Chelsea FC: £144 million*
- *Annual revenue budget for West Mercia Police Authority: £166 million*
- *Annual cost of shoplifting and retail crime to the Scottish economy: £166 million*

And what of the other England players who beat Argentina in November 2005? What is their transfer value? The record can't help. When Sol Campbell went from Spurs to Arsenal, he went for nothing. And last time David James and Michael Carrick changed clubs, the fees were undisclosed. (The time before last, they sold for just £3.5 million and £3 million respectively. One suspects they were a little more expensive last time.)

Let's assume that the average price of these other players (Campbell, James, Carrick, King, Gerrard, Green and Terry) is the same as for the 16 players above.

ii. Based on these figures, what is the combined transfer value of the entire 23 England players on the squad for the team that played Argentina?

a) £238.0 million
b) £300.6 million
c) £135.0 million

Answers: i) a ii) a

A league game was first broadcast on the radio in 1927.

- *Estimated price paid by Malcolm Glazer for control of Manchester United: £790 million*
- *Annual budget for the BBC World Service: £225 million*

Just where is West Mercia anyway?

Balls

Stilton comes from Stilton, Champagne comes from Champagne, Taramasalata comes from Taramasalata. Sorry, no, scrap that last one. And footballs? Footballs most frequently come from the villages around Sialkot in Pakistan, a place generally considered the global capital of the football-stitching world ...

US imports of soccer balls

Source country	% by value
Pakistan	71
China	19
Indonesia	5
India	1
Other	4

Source: US Department of Labor

It used to be that football stitching was an industry blighted by child slavery (like carpet making and the Côte d'Ivorian cocoa harvest). But now, thanks to the sterling efforts of brands like Reebok and organisations from FIFA down, non-governmental organisations report that to a very large extent this is no longer true.

Since 1970, the 'official' soccer ball has been of what is termed the Buckminster design (named after British design legend Buckminster Fuller), formed from 20 hexagonal and 12 pentagonal surfaces. A child experienced at stitching Buckminster balls might stitch 3 balls a day and be paid by the ball.

Recently, however, FIFA adopted a new 14-panel design from Adidas called Teamgeist™.

Since this author can only speculate on the stitching demands each different panel design represents, let's assume for argument's sake they each take as long to stitch as each other.

---

i. If a child can stitch three 32-panel balls a day, about how many 14-panel balls could she manage?

a) 11
b) 9
c) 7

A stitcher used to earn about £0.43 a ball. But nowadays, a 'Fairtrade' football carries a premium of £1.10, to 'ensure whoever stitches your ball receives a fair wage'. So you can rest assured that to bring you a ball retailing at £75.00, the stitcher will have been paid a 'fair' wage of about £1.53 a ball or £10.49 a day.

---

ii. For how many days could someone with £75 pay someone else £10.49 a day?

a) 12
b) 7
c) 22

Answers: i) c ii) b

The US football market, in which Pakistan had a 71% share by value, is worth a total of US $34 million (£19.2 million).

So, to summarise, how much labour will a single football buy? That thing the heroes of this book kick around every day for £100,000 a week? In Pakistan, it will pay a football stitcher for slightly more than 7 days of work. At Stamford Bridge, it will pay a midfielder for slightly more than 7 minutes ...

This Looks Big on Your Bum

The new Wembley stadium will seat 90,000 spectators. Assume that on average each seat has a bum-supporting area that's 40 centimetres square. An acre is 4,046.85642 square metres. Call it 4,000 square metres, which is 40 million square centimetres.

---

i. What will be the acreage of bum support at the new Wembley?

a) 3.6
b) 1.8
c) 5.4

By this measure, the entire population of the UK could be seated in the biggest park in Birmingham – the National Nature Reserve at Sutton Park.

By the by, the volume that the walls and roof of the new Wembley will enclose is 4 million cubic metres. This is about the amount of water consumed by New York City in a day. So if you want to visualise how much water a big modern city uses every day, just picture the inside of Wembley stadium.

Answer: i) a

If all the seating in the new Wembley was placed end to end, it would stretch 34 miles.

Home and Away

It's estimated that 100,000 England fans will be travelling to Germany for their little football contest. We'll assume they're all in work.

The UK working population is 28.8 million.

> ### i. How many working Brits will stay at home to watch the 2006 World Cup for every one who goes?
>
> a) 351
> b) 287
> c) 223

- *Maximum capacity of a Boeing 767: 285 seats*
- *Air fare London to Munich (single): €176.5*

Assume every fan will travel to and from Germany by air, flying between London and Munich.

> ### ii. Total potential value in air fares?
>
> a) € 20.4 million
> b) € 53.5 million
> c) € 35.3 million

- *Price Chelsea paid to Marseille for Didier Drogba: €35.5 million*

Answers: i) b ii) c

In 1930, European teams had to take a 2-week sea voyage to reach their World Cup host Uruguay.

Sickie

Various surveys suggest up to 20% of workers will take time off to watch a 2006 World Cup match when England are playing: in Britain that's 5.76 million people. During the groups stage this shouldn't be a problem, because England's games are either in the evening or at the weekend. The only potential problem from a 'work-the-buggers-until-they-drop' employer's point of view will be the game against Trinidad and Tobago, starting in Nuremberg at 6 pm German time (5 pm UK time) on Thursday 15 June.

Therefore, let's assume that 5.76 million British workers will make themselves absent for 2.5 hours of work time that day. The average British worker has a gross domestic product of about £11.88 an hour.

i. How much might England's game against Trinidad and Tobago cost the UK?
a) £89,443,000
b) £223,981,000
c) £171,072,000

- *Total value of the England squad that played Argentina in November 2005: £165.5 million*

Put another way, every worker in the entire country would have to work for nearly 2.5 hours to raise the price of a new England team – so Sven, don't lose them.

Answer: i) c

About 1 in 7 professional players will suffer a serious injury during their career.

Don't Mention the War

At the 1938 World Cup in France, victory in the Final went to Italy. Thus, when war came, it fell to an Italian Football Federation official named Ottorino Barassi to conceal the trophy for the duration, so World Cup legend has it, hidden in a shoe-box under his bed.

The original World Cup stood 35 centimetres tall. A man's UK shoe size is roughly 3 times his foot length in inches minus 22. There are 2.54 centimetres in an inch.

> **i. So what is the biggest-sized shoe that would fit a shoe-box 35 centimetres long?**
>
> a) 17
> b) 23
> c) 19

Your feet are 15.2% of your height in length. A man with feet 35 centimetres long would, therefore, be nearly 7 feet 7 inches tall.

Clearly a big bloke then Ottorino.

One Record Wayne Rooney Can't Break

Michael Owen was born on 14 December 1979. When he scored against Romania in France on 22 June 1998, he became the youngest ever player to score for England in the World Cup. He was 6,765 days old.

Answer: i) c

Up to 60% of players will develop Anterior Ankle Impingement Syndrome (Footballer's Ankle).

Wayne Rooney was born on 24 October 1985.

> ### i. What will Wayne's age be in days on 10 June 2006?
>
> a) 8834
> b) 8134
> c) 7534

- *10 June 2006 is the date of England's first World Cup group game against Paraguay.*

So who's the daddy?

(To date, the youngest player ever to play in the World Cup was Norman Whiteside for Northern Ireland against Yugoslavia in 1982. He was 17 years 42 days. The oldest was Cameroon's Roger Milla, who scored against Russia in 1994 when he was 42 years 39 days.)

It Starts in Munich and it Ends in Berlin

A total of a million overseas fans are expected in Germany for the 2006 World Cup.

On 9 June, the first day, there's a match in Munich and another in Gelsenkirchen.

Assume half the arriving overseas fans will enter Germany at Munich airport and half at Düsseldorf, the nearest airport to Gelsenkirchen.

Answer: i) c

Sir Stanley Matthews' last international was against Denmark, aged 42 years 103 days. He didn't score.

(For the purpose of this Football Freak we'll assume nobody will be arriving by road or sea. Unrealistic? Certainly – but we're only Football Freaking ...)

Munich airport handles 24,953,000 passengers a year (365 days). Düsseldorf airport handles 14,124,000 in the same period.

> ### i. How long does Munich airport usually take to process 500,000 passengers?
>
> a) 12.6 days
> b) 7.4 days
> c) 3.0 days

> ### ii. How long does Düsseldorf airport usually take to process 500,000 passengers?
>
> a) 8.7 days
> b) 12.9 days
> c) 17.4 days

So if you're going to a match on 9 June you may need to set off a bit early ...

The German for Headache is *Kopfschmerzen*

They have a lot of beer in Germany. If you want some, here is the address of the Löwenbräu bierkeller in Munich.

Answers: i) b ii) b

German airports handle 121 million passengers a year.

Löwenbräukeller
Nymphenburgerstr. 2,
80335 München-Neuhausen.
Phone: +49 (0) 89 52 60 21
Fax: +49 (0) 89 52 89 33
www.loewenbraeukeller.com

You should get a seat there; reputedly, it has room for more than 1,000.

And while we're on the subject: they make a lot of fuss about beer in Germany.

Take the *Reinheitsgebot*. Oft claimed as Germany's oldest surviving law, the *Reinheitsgebot* was drawn up by a Bavarian Duke in April 1516 and finally lifted in 1987. It limited beer ingredients to malted grain, hops, water and later, yeast.

If you believe the PR, this is what guarantees the quality of German beer ...

But in reality, it doesn't now and it never did. In fact the law was only enacted to control which grains could be brewed and which baked. There's nothing in the *Reinheitsgebot* that guarantees your beer won't be dishwater, just that it'll be pure dish-water. Indeed, despite its medieval claims the *Reinheitsgebot* didn't apply throughout Germany until 1906 – when, before signing up to a unified German state, Bavaria insisted the *Reinheitsgebot* be enforced nationwide.

The average German drinks 120 litres of beer a year, the average Brit 104 litres (about half a pint a day) and the average Aussie 109 litres.

Assume that for the month of the 2006 World Cup, the average England fan will quaff rather than quench and drink 6 times what they normally would.

i. How many extra litres of beer will the Germans need to brew to satisfy 100,000 Brits for a month?

a) 5,200,000
b) 7,100,000
c) 9,000,000

Although some German brewers still see the *Reinheitsgebot* as a valuable marketing tool, an increasing number pay it little regard nowadays; furthermore, it doesn't apply to foreign brands.

And what has this got to do with football? Rights, money and profit: Budweiser multinational Anheuser-Busch was initially licensed to sell beer in and around World Cup venues for €33.4 million. The deal was a monopoly that completely excluded local brewers; a glimpse of the seamless link between the globalisation of 'stuff' and the globalisation of football.

But then the wheeler-dealers from Germany met with the wheeler-dealers from Anheuser-Busch and pretty soon they'd hammered out a new deal that resolved things to everyone's satisfaction: the Germans got the right to carry on selling beer in their own country during the tournament, but lost the right to stop Anheuser-Busch from doing the same thing afterwards.

(Football Freaking is the art of doodling with numbers – just for fun.)

Stick

The population of Germany is 82,431,390.

There are 262 police officers per 100,000 German people.

Answer: i) a
The 1982 European Cup Final reputedly saw 10,000 Aston Villa fans tricked into drinking alcohol-free lager.

100,000 England fans are expected to travel to the tournament.

> **i. So how many German police officers await each England fan?**
>
> a) 34.56
> b) 8.64
> c) 2.16

No contest.

Here We Go

The big showcase opening game at the 2006 World Cup will be Germany vs. Costa Rica in the München Allianz Arena otherwise known – because stadium name sponsorship isn't allowed – as the FIFA World Cup Stadium Munich, which turns red when Bayern München play at home and blue for TSV 1860 München. On 9 June 2005, Munich was windy, 11 degrees Celsius and there was drizzle. Hope it's nicer in 2006. The game starts at 6 pm. Take underground U6 to 'Fröttmaning'.

And what of Germany's chances? Last time there was a World Cup Final in Munich, on 7 July 1974, the Netherlands took a penalty off West Germany within 2 minutes, then lost the game 2:1 by half time.

Germany has an impressive record in the World Cup finals. In the 17 competitions before 2006, they qualified for the finals 15 times and won the cup thrice. Of the remaining dozen, they lost in the actual final 4 times, the semis 3 times (and came third once), and the quarters 3 times too. And they haven't been knocked out in the first round since 1938. In fact, of the

---

Answer: i) c

1,072 England hooligans were banned from travelling to the 2002 World Cup.

90 games German teams have ever played in the finals stage of the World Cup, they've only lost 19 games (one of which was an East/West German derby) and been drawn 20 times at 90 minutes. Remove all World Cup games involving East Germany from the record and Germany have only lost 16 games out of 84; less than 1 in 5.

And here they are ...

1934	Czechoslovakia vs. Germany	3:1
1938	Switzerland vs. Germany	4:2
1954	Hungary vs. Germany FR	8:3
1958	Sweden vs. Germany FR	3:1
1958	France vs. Germany FR	6:3
1962	Yugoslavia vs. Germany FR	1:0
1966	England vs. Germany FR	4:2
1970	Italy vs. Germany FR	4:3
1978	Austria vs. Germany FR	3:2
1982	Algeria vs. Germany FR	2:1
1982	Italy vs. Germany FR	3:1
1986	Denmark vs. Germany FR	2:0
1986	Argentina vs. Germany FR	3:2
1994	Bulgaria vs. Germany	2:1
1998	Croatia vs. Germany	3:0
2002	Brazil vs. Germany	2:0

i. Which of the following scores is closest to Germany's average losing score?

a) 3:2
b) 3:1
c) 4:1

Hard to beat the Germans ...

Answer: i) b

483,000 fans attended the 1938 World Cup.

Or Rather, Here *They* Go ...

As to wins or draws in the World Cup finals, Germany (West, East and reunified) have won or drawn a total of 72 games ... or far too many to list here. The critical thing is that Germany today isn't the Germany that was – before the 1994 World Cup, Germany was a nation divided. So let's look solely at the 11 games Germany has so far won in the World Cup finals post-reunification.

Here they are ...

1994	Germany vs. Bolivia	1:0
1994	Germany vs. Korea Republic	3:2
1994	Germany vs. Belgium	3:2
1998	Germany vs. USA	2:0
1998	Germany vs. Iran	2:0
1998	Germany vs. Mexico	2:1

- *Apologies to Eire for avoiding this chance to include their 1:1 draw with Germany in 2002.*

2002	Germany vs. Saudi Arabia	8:0
2002	Germany vs. Cameroon	2:0
2002	Germany vs. Paraguay	1:0
2002	Germany vs. USA	1:0
2002	Germany vs. South Korea	1:0

i. Which of the following scores is closest to Germany's average winning score?

a) 2:0
b) 2:1
c) 3:1

Clinical demolition.

Support Act

The 'B movie' game on the opening day of the 2006 World Cup is between Poland and Ecuador.

History? They've met once before when Poland trounced Ecuador 3:0.

	FIFA rank	Population	Per capita GDP	3F
Poland	23	38,557,984	10,015	2.19
Ecuador	37	13,363,593	3,090	23.56

Kick-off is at 9 pm. In Gelsenkirchen (at the Arena Auf Schalke, sorry, FIFA World Cup Stadium Gelsenkirchen). Go 395 miles NNW up and to the left a bit from Munich and there you are. You need to take tram 302 from the main station. Head towards Gelsenkirchen Buer Rathaus, to Veltins Arena Auf Schalke.

The weather in Gelsenkirchen was better than in Munich on the same day in 2005 – 14 degrees Celsius with a pleasant breeze ... But don't expect much. First day matches are rarely that electric.

Football Freaking Forecast? Poland will win 2:1.

In 40% of the 40 games that have ever been played on World Cup opening days, no side has scored more than 1 goal.

Results from the opening day's games at every World Cup finals					
2002	Senegal vs. France	1:0	1954	Hungary vs. Wales	1:1
1998	Morocco vs. Norway	2:2	1954	Sweden vs. Mexico	3:0
1998	Brazil vs. Scotland	2:1	1954	Soviet Union vs. England	2:2
1994	Spain vs. Korea Republic	2:2	1954	Brazil vs. Austria	3:0
1994	Germany vs. Bolivia	1:0	1954	Brazil vs. Mexico	5:0
1990	Cameroon vs. Argentina	1:0	1950	Yugoslavia vs. France	1:0
1986	Bulgaria vs. Italy	1:1	1950	Austria vs. Scotland	1:0

continued overleaf

Results from the opening day's games at every World Cup finals *continued*

1982	Belgium vs. Argentina	1:0	1950	Uruguay vs. Czechoslovakia	2:0
1978	Germany FR vs. Poland	0:0	1950	Brazil vs. Mexico	4:0
1974	Brazil vs. Yugoslavia	0:0	1938	Switzerland vs. Germany	1:1
1970	Mexico vs. Soviet Union	0:0	1934	Austria vs. France	3:2
1966	England vs. Uruguay	0:0	1934	Italy vs. USA	7:1
1962	Uruguay vs. Colombia	2:1	1934	Germany vs. Belgium	5:2
1962	Chile vs. Switzerland	3:1	1934	Czechoslovakia vs. Romania	2:1
1962	Brazil vs. Mexico	2:0	1934	Switzerland vs. Netherlands	3:2
1962	Argentina vs. Bulgaria	1:0	1934	Sweden vs. Argentina	3:2
1958	N. Ireland vs. Czechoslovakia	1:0	1934	Spain vs. Brazil	3:1
1958	Germany FR vs. Argentina	3:1	1934	Hungary vs. Egypt	4:2
1958	Yugoslavia vs. Scotland	1:1	1930	France vs. Mexico	4:1
1958	France vs. Paraguay	7:3	1930	USA vs. Belgium	3:0

i. Which of the following scores is closest to the average score at first day games at the World Cup?

a) 2:1
b) 2:0
c) 1:1

- *Even this score is artificially high thanks to the high-scoring preliminaries from Day One of the 1934 World Cup.*

Germany's average score in losing games at the World Cup is about 3:1. The average score for games lost on the first day of the World Cup is about 2:1 or less. The average score by which Germany have won games in the World Cup finals since reunification? About 2:0.

Football Freaking's conclusion? A German win on Day One should be a certainty.

Answer: i) a

395,000 fans attended the 1934 World Cup.

1934

The second ever World Cup was hosted by the kingdom of Italy in 1934, a land in thrall to Benito Mussolini – its dictator since 1922. At the tournament (the first in which participating teams had to qualify) it's said that Il Duce's influence went so far as to dictate, as dictators do, the choice of referees for Italy's games. Ivan Eklind, the Swede who refereed both Italy's 1:0 semi-final win against Austria in Milan and their 2:1 victory over Czechoslovakia in the Rome final, was alleged to have met privately with Mussolini before the matches to 'discuss' the games. Rene Mercet, the Swiss referee who adjudicated over Italy's replayed quarter-final defeat of Spain, which Italy won 1:0, was considered to have been so partisan that after the tournament he was suspended from the Swiss league.

All of which ought to add zest to Italy vs. Czech Republic in Hamburg on 22 June 2006. But it won't: Italy has morphed into a republic since 1934 and the Czech Republic has divorced Slovakia. It's a difficult match to call: 5 previous encounters, 2 wins each and 1 draw; the aggregate score is 7:6 to Italy.

The Football Freaking figures for this fixture are contradictory too: despite Italy's population and infrastructure (and Karel Bruckner the Czech coach naming Italy as the group favourite), it's the Czechs who FIFA currently rank (at the time of writing) as second in the world while Italy languish at 12th position. Sometimes the numbers can't tell us everything.

	FIFA Rank	Population	Per capita GDP (€)	3F
Italy	12	58,103,033	23,120	1.17
Czech Republic	2	10,241,138	14,780	1.50

For what could be one of the most cracking games of the tournament, the Football Freaking Forecast is a 2:2 draw.

The 9 finals games in the 1934 World Cup were altogether more sedentary than the 8 preliminary games, which saw 43 goals. Here are the results from the finals.

Match	Score
Italy vs. Spain	1:1
Austria vs. Hungary	2:1
Czechoslovakia vs. Switzerland	3:2
Germany vs. Sweden	2:1
Italy vs. Spain	1:0
Czechoslovakia vs. Germany	3:1
Italy vs. Austria	1:0
Germany vs. Austria	3:2
Italy vs. Czechoslovakia	2:1

i. Which of the following scores is closest to the average score of finals games at the 1934 World Cup?

a) 2:0
b) 2:1
c) 1:0

These 9 games saw just 27 goals: a drop from more than 5 goals a match to just 3 over a single round. What happened? Impossible to tell when there are bent refs afoot ...

Something to Discuss Over Your Bier

Fast forward 72 years to Germany – and Bundesliga referee Robert Hoyzer has been jailed for rigging matches and pocketing thousands at the behest of Croatian gamblers.

The first result Hoyzer claims he fixed was a friendly between Middlesbrough FC and Hansa Rostock that the Boro lost 3:1. Later, in the German Cup, he gave regional side Paderborn a surprise victory over first division Hamburg SV – by giving the latter team a red card and 2 dubious penalties – a result for which prosecutors say he received €20,000.

i. There are 64 games in a World Cup nowadays. At €20,000 a match, how much would it cost to fix the contest?

a) €128,000
b) €12,800,000
c) €1,280,000

Sounds like a bargain ... One of the Croat gamblers on whose behalf Hoyzer acted, allegedly earned at least €730,000 from the Paderborn vs. Hamburg SV match.

ii. With an illicit €730,000 up for grabs each game, how much could be earned from 64 World Cup games?

a) €467,200
b) €4,672,000
c) €46,720,000

Sounds like a real bargain ...

Answers: i) c ii) c

Robert Hoyzer is reportedly 6′ 5″ tall.

The aftershock from Hoyzer's disgrace is being felt around Europe; investigators probe for betting scams in Britain. Clearly the spectre of match fixing may well be an issue at the 2006 World Cup. And maybe in 2010 as well. Since winning the right to host the 2010 World Cup, South African football has been plagued by a match-fixing scandal in which a cartel of crooked referees are accused of taking bribes. Watch this space ...

After the Oompah-Pahs are Over

So what of the big opening game in 2006: Germany vs. Costa Rica?

	FIFA Rank	Population	Per capita GDP	3F
Germany	16	82,431,390	23,950	---
Costa Rica	21	4,016,173	8,010	6.53

On every dimension from population and GDP to FIFA rank and even 3F, you'd tip Germany for a win and so the Football Freaking Forecast for this match is, indeed, a dull 2:0 win to Germany ...

There is, however, no match history to confirm this by, as the German team and the Costa Rican team have never met. But this isn't to say there's no relationship between the two.

Throughout the 1990s, Germany provided Costa Rica with support in the field of financial and technical cooperation. The total value of German cooperation was approximately €123 million (US $147 million/£83 million).

Costa Rica's population is 4,016,173. So over the decade, Germany effectively gave every man, woman and child in Costa Rica about $36.60, which is 5 Costa Rican colon or about one US cent per day each.

Could anyone seriously suggest some kind of bribery had gone on here? Of course not: if Germany beat Costa Rica in the opening game it will be entirely because they're the better team.

And what if Germany decided to provide $36.60 (£20.66) in 'assistance' to the entire populations of every country *Football Freaking* confidently predicts Germany might meet in the 2006 World Cup?

Here are those teams and the populations that back them ...

Team	Population	Team	Population
Sweden	9,001,774	Costa Rica	4,016,173
Poland	38,557,984	Netherlands	16,407,491
Ecuador	13,363,593	France	60,656,178
England	50,598,940	Argentina	39,537,943
	Total combined population	232,140,076	

i. How much would it cost to give 242,140,076 people £20.66 each?

a) £2.9 billion/€4.3 billion
b) £4.0 billion/€2.7 billion
c) £4.8 billion/€7.1 billion

- *Combined annual purchasing power of German boys aged 15-19 years: €7.5 billion/£5.1 billion*

Answer: i) c

The Federación Costarricense de Fútbol was founded in 1921.

ME. Let's Talk Some More About ME.

At the time of writing, there are 5,995 books about This-Ball-We-Call-Foot listed on Amazon UK. Of these, 1,361 are categorised as biographies and 59 of these are about David Beckham. This is more than the total number of biographies listed for Brad Pitt (15), Tom Cruise (18) and Frank Sinatra (23) combined. However, though he may dwarf superstars like Tom Cruise and Frank Sinatra, David is only an amateur on the having-books-written-about-you front compared with, say, Tiger Woods. Though 8 months younger than Beckham, Tiger's already been profiled 182 times – and he doesn't have the celebrity missus. And compared with Elvis, the subject of a staggering 1,447 separate biographies? David is just a beginner.

> ### i. How many times more biographies are there about Elvis than Becks?
>
> a) 34.5
> b) 14.5
> c) 24.5

Exactly how many books are listed on Amazon UK? Well, who could be bothered to count – except Amazon of course ... Suffice to say, the last football book in order of sales, the 5,995th, ranking 485,224th overall, is called *Watford Season by Season: A Detailed Record Of More Than 4000 Matches From 1881/82* (by Trefor Jones, with a forward by Graham Taylor). Now this isn't *Football Freaking*, this isn't *Number Freaking*, no, this is what you call a labour of love. And suspect grammar: that 'from' should be a 'since'. But we are picking nits. Trefor Jones? *Football Freaking* salutes you as football's number one fan.

Answer: i) c

The number one football book and biography at the time of writing is Robbie Fowler's *Fowler: My Biography*.

(And finally – on what many England fans may find a more satisfying personal note – at the time of writing, the least popular book in the football biography list – at number 1,361 – profiles Diego Maradona.)

Football Really is War

The shortest war ever recorded was between Britain and Zanzibar and lasted from 9.02 am until 9.40 am on Thursday, 27 August 1896. So, when Andy Cole slotted one in against Newcastle in the 38th minute of their 3:0 thumping by Manchester City on Wednesday, 1 February 2006, if he'd been fighting the Zanzibarians in 1896 for as long as it'd been since kick-off, the hostilities would have been virtually over ... And by the way Zanzibar – sorry.

There are two famous facts, in Britain at least, about football and war. The first is that on Christmas Day 1914, British and German troops emerged from their trenches and played football in no man's land. (Indeed, there may have been several games.) In the most famous account, a German officer, a Leutnant Johannes Niemann of the 133rd Royal Saxon Regiment, recalls a game he played in against the Scottish Seaforth Highlanders, which the Germans won 3:2. On penalties presumably.

Britain entered the First World War on 4 August 1914. It ended 1,560 days later on 11 November 1918.

i. How many 90-minute football games could be played one after the other in 1,560 days?
a) 12,480
b) 18,720
c) 24,960

Answer: i) c
In 6 days you could play 96 90-minute football games one after the other.

For two sides to compete in 24,960 games – each sending a squad of 23 different men to each game – would require 574,080 men from each country. During the First World War, Germany mobilised 11 million troops and Britain deployed 5.4 million.

> **ii. Given these troop sizes, how many 90-minute games could Britain and Germany have played simultaneously for the entire duration of the First World War, never selecting the same men twice?**
>
> a) 4
> b) 9
> c) 14

Would it have been any more stupid than killing or breaking 15,142,000 people?

The second 'fact' people know is that somewhere, sometime, in South America there was once a war about football. And there was ... kind of. For 6 days between 14 July and 20 July 1969, El Salvador and Honduras fought a war along their mutual border in a territorial dispute. A ceasefire was rapidly negotiated. From a historic point of view, the war is noteworthy, apparently, as the last time Second World War aircraft were used in action.

This war's connection to football is that the bubbling resentment between the two nations was exacerbated by riots between 6 June and 27 June 1969 (a few weeks before the hostilities began) during the second preliminary round of the 1970 World Cup in Mexico.

Ultimately, El Salvador defeated Honduras in the football by an aggregate score of 6:3.

Answer: ii) b

In 1997, a programme from the 1915 Khaki Cup Final during the First World War sold for £11,000.

So did winning at football inspire El Salvador to attack Honduras or did losing at football oblige Honduras to attack El Salvador? Turns out it was El Salvador's army who launched the 1969 attack against Honduras – on 14 July ... which proves it's winners you have to watch, not the losers.

Football is Played the Length of Britain and All Around the World

It's been calculated (apparently) that the average distance covered collectively by the players in each team in a Premiership game is 69.8 miles.

The 20 Premiership teams between them play 380 games in a full season.

> ### i. So how many miles do the teams cover between them in a Premiership season?
>
> a) 42,778
> b) 53,048
> c) 89,012

- *Circumference of the Earth: 24,901 miles*

This figure of 69.8 miles includes (apparently) an increase of 2.3 miles per team per game over the previous two seasons. Let's assume (after all, Football Freaking is all about assumptions) that the increase over the previous season alone was half that – 1.15 miles per team per game.

Over 380 games, this amounts to an increase of 874 miles – the distance from Land's End to John O'Groats. Like the title says: football is played the length of Britain and all around the world.

Answer: i) b

The first ever league hat-trick was by Walter Tait when Burnley beat Bolton 3:4 on 15 September 1888.

And it Makes You Fit as a Flea (Almost)

So 11 players (yes, we have to include the goalie) cover 69.8 miles playing for a nominal period of 90 minutes (we'll ignore red cards and regard the net impact of substitutions as 0).

i. On average, at what speed does each player play?

a) 5.78 mph
b) 8.88 mph
c) 4.23 mph

- *Jump velocity of the common flea* (Pulex irritans)*: 4.5 mph*

Or a mile each, every 14 minutes 11 seconds.

And if both sides run 69.8 miles each, that's a combined total of 139.6 miles (roughly the distance from Manchester to Bristol). And how fast would you have to travel to cover that distance in 90 minutes? 93 mph.

So 93 mph is the net speed of a football match ...

On Fields of Dreams

When was the last time Sol Campbell took off his jacket and rolled it into a ball for a makeshift goalpost? When was the last time Michael Owen made a pile with all the stuff in his pockets for another? (No idea myself; just thought you might know ...)

The rules of the game dictate that the pitch must be between 100 and 130 yards long and 50 and 100 yards wide.

Answer: i) c

93 mph is the wind speed of the synonymous level one Atlantic hurricane and category one Pacific typhoon.

Below are the dimensions of every pitch in the English Premiership.

Club	Pitch dimensions (yards)	Area (square yards)	Club	Pitch dimensions (yards)	Area (square yards)
Manchester City	116.5 x 78	9,087	Portsmouth	115.0 x 73	8,395
Manchester United	116.0 x 76	8,816	Chelsea	113.0 x 74	8,362
Blackburn Rovers	115.0 x 76	8,740	Aston Villa	115.0 x 72	8,280
Everton	112.0 x 78	8,736	Fulham	110.0 x 75	8,250
Birmingham City	115.0 x 75	8,625	Liverpool	110.0 x 75	8,250
Middlesbrough	115.0 x 75	8,625	Charlton Athletic	112.0 x 73	8,176
Sunderland	115.0 x 75	8,625	West Ham United	112.0 x 72	8,064
Wigan Athletic	115.0 x 75	8,625	Newcastle United	110.0 x 73	8,030
West Bromwich Albion	115.0 x 74	8,510	Tottenham Hotspur	110.0 x 73	8,030
Bolton Wanderers	114.0 x 74	8,436	Arsenal (Highbury)	110.0 x 71	7,810

i. What is the total area of Premiership pitches in England?

a) 145,365 square yards (121,544 square metres)
b) 188,923 square yards (157,963 square metres)
c) 168,472 square yards (140,864 square metres)

- *Area of the gardens around Buckingham Palace: 160,000 square metres/ 191,358 square yards*

Based on these touchline lengths, the average Premiership pitch is about 113.28 x 74.35 yards: slightly bigger than Stamford Bridge, slightly smaller than the Reebok Stadium.

- *Area of the Wembley Stadium pitch: 8,625 yards*

Answer: i) c

Wembley Stadium was originally slated to cost £757 million. Ha!

ii. At the average playing speed of 4.23 mph, how long does it take to cover 113.28 yards?

a) 43 seconds
b) 55 seconds
c) 71 seconds

So our Football Freaking conclusion? After a goal in the Premiership, any uninjured player not back in their position in their own half, ready to start, after about 1 minute is demonstrably time-wasting ...

Astro-Hallowed-Turf

Astroturf currently retails at £450 for 17.41 square yards.

The average size of an English Premiership pitch is 113.28 x 74.35 yards.

Assume the people who fit Astroturf are synthetic lawn gods who never waste a single square inch.

i. How much would it cost to Astroturf an average Premiership pitch?

a) £108,771
b) £217,695
c) £435,084

- *Cost of Astroturf to cover a garden area 50 x 20 feet: £2,872 pro-rata*

- *Cost of Astroturf to cover every pitch in the English Premiership (168,472 square yards): £4,354,532*

Answers: ii) b i) b

To Astroturf Wembley would cost £5,237 more than for an average FA pitch.

Welcome to Bologna on Capital Gold for England Vs. San Marino with Tennents' Pilsner Brewed with Czechoslovakian Yeast for that Extra Pilsner Taste; and England are 1 Down ...

Bologna. November 1993. World Cup qualifying game for USA 1994. England trounce tiny San Marino 7:1 ... But not until after Davide Gualtieri scores the fastest goal in the history of the competition to give San Marino the lead after just 8.3 seconds ...

Since we know that much more and it's time-wasting, we'll assume it should take an average of 60 seconds on the clock to restart a game after a goal ...

i. How many goals could be scored in 90 minutes if they took 8.3 seconds each?

a) 45
b) 61
c) 79

By comparison, the fastest goal in the UEFA Champions League was by Gilberto Silva for Arsenal at PSV Eindhoven on 25 September 2002 – he scored in 20.07 seconds.

Again we'll allow 60 seconds after each goal for play to resume.

Answer: i) c

The fastest World Cup finals goal was in 2002 when Turkey scored in 11 seconds against Korea Republic.

> **ii. How many goals could be scored in 90 minutes if they took 20.07 seconds each?**
>
> a) 56
> b) 68
> c) 80

It takes about 8.3 seconds to announce: 'Welcome to Bologna on Capital Gold for England vs. San Marino with Tennents' Pilsner brewed with Czechoslovakian yeast for that extra Pilsner taste; and England are 1 down ...'

You Win or You Lose. There's No In Between.

The most comprehensive thrashing ever in an international competition came during the qualifiers for the 2002 World Cup, when Australia beat American Samoa 31:0 in April 2001.

(This result presumably condemns American Samoan goalie Nicky Salapu to the record books as the worst-ever international goalkeeper for several years to come.)

Three days earlier, Australia set the previous international record for tonking with 22 goals against Tonga. But their match against American Samoa made that victory look slim.

The first 30 Australian goals occurred within the normal 90-minute run of play, while the final goal was scored during stoppage time at the end of the second half.

Assume it takes 60 seconds to restart a game after a goal.

Answer: ii) b

American Samoa's greatest victory was their 3:0 defeat of the Wallis and Futuna Islands in 1983.

i. On average, how often did Australia slot a goal in during the normal 90 minutes of the game?

a) 2¼ minutes
b) 3 minutes
c) 4¾ minutes

In fact, Australia's goals are recorded as having been scored as follows.

Note: there was no score during the first 7 minutes of the first half or the first 4 of the second. Take this into account and those 30 goals came in 79 minutes or once every 2 minutes 38 seconds.

Game period	Minutes	Australia's scoring moments
First half	0–15	8' 11' 12' 14'
	16–30	17' 19' 20' 23' 26' 27' 29'
	31–45	32' 33' 37' 42' 45'
Second half	46–60	50' 52' 54' 56' 58'
	61–75	62' 65' 67'
	76–90	79' 80' 82' 85' 87' 90'
Stoppage time	90+	90+

Clearly it was quite a game. To be fair to American Samoa, FIFA bureaucracy allowed only one player from the regular squad to play. The top scorer was Socceroo striker Archie Thompson, who notched up 13 goals and a world record. His goals are underlined in the list. Apparently the 31:0 score was first reported wrongly as 32:0, but corrected later: which must have made it feel much less embarrassing.

In just 13 minutes during the second quarter-hour of the first half there were 7 goals. Or 1 every 1 minute 52 seconds (112 seconds).

Answer: i) b
When a touring English FA XI beat Australia 17:0 in 1951, Australia's goalie was named Norman Conquest.

ii. Averaging 1 goal every 112 seconds, how many times would you score in 90 minutes?

a) 38
b) 48
c) 58

A lot less than 68 or 79.

In the 4 games they played in the Oceania Group One qualifying stage, Australia scored a total of 66 goals: including the 31 against American Samoa and 22 against Tonga, plus another 11 against Samoa and 2 against Fiji – who themselves scored 27 goals in their run for a qualifying place. After the group stage, Australia went on to beat New Zealand 6:1 on aggregate, but then lost 3:1 on aggregate to Uraguay. A mistake they made sure not to repeat in 2005 ...

Don't you just wish it could be like this in the Nationwide Conference?

Best Effort

The highest score ever in a European Cup game was in 1969/70 in a first round first leg match, when the Dutch team Feyenoord beat the Icelandic team K R Reykjavik 12:0. The highest aggregate score, meanwhile, came in the preliminary round of 1965/66 when Portuguese side Benfica beat Luxembourgese team Dudelange by a total of 18:0.

Presumably, we can safely assume the Feyenoord vs. K R Reykjavik game didn't go beyond 90 minutes ...

Answer: ii) b

The Icelandic national stadium, Laugardalsvöllur, normally seats just 7,000 people.

i. On average, how long did it take Feyenoord to score each goal?

a) 7.5 minutes
b) 6.1 minutes
c) 9.2 minutes

In the UEFA Champions League, the highest aggregate score was in a match between AS Monaco and La Coruna on bonfire night 2003 – it went 8:3 to AS Monaco by the final whistle ...

London to New York Marathon

It is a truth universally acknowledged that an Arsenal in possession of a good unbeaten run must be in want of a beating. And so it was in October 2004 that Manchester United brought Arsenal's 49-game unbeaten run – the longest in English Premiership history – to an end, when Ruud Van Nistelrooy scored a penalty after 72 minutes.

Arsenal's run began in May 2003. At that time, on average, teams ran 67.5 miles in a game. Though this figure probably improved, for the sake of this Football Freak, we'll assume this was how far Arsenal's opponents were running on average for every game throughout Arsenal's record unbeaten streak (and, pro rata, for the first 72 minutes of the 90-minute game, 50 miles).

i. How far did Arsenal's opponents run between them before Arsenal took their fall?

a) 2,871.6 miles
b) 3,361.5 miles
c) 4,216.7 miles

Answers: i) a i) b

Monaco hasn't yet joined FIFA or UEFA. In 2001, the national side played its first ever international, beating Tibet 2:1.

- *Distance from London to New York: 3,458 miles*
- *Length of Ireland's national road network: 3,355 miles*

The Arsenal pitch is 110 yards long and there are 1,760 yards in a mile.

> **ii. How many of these pitch lengths did Arsenal's opponents run as they clocked up 3,361.5 miles?**
>
> a) 53,784
> b) 48,322
> c) 61,989

Of the 20 longest unbeaten runs since 1993, over a third (7) were by Manchester United, and a quarter (5) were by Arsenal. Clearly there's some history here ...

The best 'clean-sheet' run (i.e. not conceding a goal) in the World Cup was in Italy in 1990, when the Italians managed 517 minutes, thanks to goalie Walter Zenga, before they conceded a goal – in the 67th minute of the semi-final (which they lost 4:3 to Argentina in a penalty shoot-out). Assuming each side runs 60 miles in a game (16 years ago even international sides were a lot less fit), Italy's opponents had to run 345 miles between them (further than London to Penzance) to slot a single goal in.

What He's Got is Legs, Which the Other Midfielders Don't Have

Based on the distance he covers in an entire match, Wayne Rooney plays football at an average speed of 4.9 mph for the entire game. This compares to an average for Premiership players of 4.23 mph.

Answer: ii) a

Between 1915 and 1917 Celtic went 62 games without a defeat.

The pitch at Old Trafford is 116 yards long. In case you've forgotten, there are 1,760 yards in a mile.

> **i. On average, how long should it take Wayne to run from the centre spot to the goal line?**
>
> a) 17.8 seconds
> b) 31.6 seconds
> c) 24.2 seconds

24.2 seconds is about how long it would take you to read the information before this question aloud.

But of course, in reality he's much faster than that: Wayne Rooney has a top speed of over 21.9 mph – that's equal to a $2^3/_4$ minute mile or a 100m in 10.2 seconds. At this speed he covers half the length of Old Trafford in about 5.4 seconds.

And that's about how long it takes to read this sentence (you're reading) out aloud.

Goalmouth Scramble

Dave from Brighton asks: 'How many goals are scored in the last 5 minutes of a game?' Well Dave, *Football Freaking* is pleased to help ...

Number Freakers are nothing if not lazy. So, we could analyse every game in every British league since the FA was founded in 1863 ... or we could just find a suitable statistical sample and extrapolate from there.

Answer: i) c

Old Trafford is reputedly worth £200 million.

Here is a 'timetable' of the goals scored during the 64 games of the 2002 World Cup.

Excluding goals scored in stoppage time or after the end of 90 minutes, there were a total of 151 goals.

Minutes passed	Goals scored in 5 minutes	Goals scored in 10 minutes	Goals scored in 15 minutes	Goals scored in 30 minutes	Goals scored in 45 minutes
0–5	9	19	26	45	65
6–10	10				
11–15	7	13			
16–20	6		19		
21–25	6	13			
26–30	7				
31–35	5	15	20	47	
36–40	10				
41–45	5	13			
46–50	8		27		86
51–55	9	19			
56–60	10				
61–65	15	23	31	59	
66–70	8				
71–75	8	14			
76–80	6		28		
81–85	9	22			
86–90	13				

Assume these numbers are indicative of first-class football in general.

i. Which is the most likely period of a game for a goal to be scored?

a) The first 20 minutes in the first half
b) The first 20 minutes in the second half
c) The last 20 minutes of 90-minute play

Answer: i) b

Football matches were first limited to 90 minutes in 1877.

Almost 28% of goals are scored at this time. This compares to just 16% scored, on average, during the quietest period of the game.

And the answer to Dave's question? Based on this sample, 8.6% of goals are scored in the last 5 minutes of the game (about 1 in 12 goals).

2:0 is a Cricket Score in Italy

Now another question, this time from young Lindsay Kennard from Dunblaine in Scotland who wants to know, what's the most common score in a football match?

Well Lindsay, yet again *Football Freaking* is happy to help: let's use the results from all 64 games in the 2002 World Cup again. This time we'll include goals scored within the first 90 minutes including stoppage time at the end of the first half.

Score	How often?	Score	How often?
0:0	4	3:1	4
1:0	14	3:2	4
1:1	12	3:3	1
2:0	10	4:0	2
2:1	6	5:2	1
2:2	2	8:0	1
3:0	3		

So Lindsay, based on these figures, the answer to your question would appear to be 1:0.

Now, assume again that these numbers are indicative of first-class football in general. (And that in this particular Football Freak, percentages are calculated by multiplying 'How often?' by approximately 1.57).

> ### i. What percentage of games end 1:0 after 90 minutes?
>
> a) 34%
> b) 22%
> c) 28%

- *The goal tally after 90 minutes in an FA Cup Final hasn't exceeded 4 since 1981.*

Hope that answers your question, Lindsay.

Sometimes in Football You Have to Score Goals

Lindsay's next question is whether there's usually only 1 goal in a game.

To work this out, we'll use the 64 games in the 2002 World Cup again. Like last time, we'll only include goals scored within the first 90 minutes including stoppage time at the end of the first half – but this time, we'll list the total number of goals in a game by the number of times it happened. (So, for example, we'll combine games ending 1:1 and 2:0 because they both had 2 goals.)

Total number of goals	How many matches	Total number of goals	How many matches
0	4	5	4
1	14	6	1
2	22	7	1
3	9	8	1
4	8		

Well, it's clear that in order of frequency there are 2 goals in a match, then only 1 goal, and then 3 or 4. What is interesting, is that you were as likely to

Answer: i) b

Out of the 124 FA Cup finals to date, 38 (about 30%) have ended 1:0.

see no goals in a World Cup match in 2002 as you were 5. At the time of writing, only time will tell if this holds true in Germany 2006. If you're reading this book and Germany 2006 is over, it's a Football Freak you can maybe research and work out for yourself ...

(In the preliminary rounds of the 2006 World Cup there were 2,464 goals in 847 games.)

In fact, during the 169,708 games played in the various English leagues since 1888, there have been 495,136 goals.

i. How many goals a game is this on average?

a) 2.92
b) 1.55
c) 3.22

Under the old league system, from 1888 to 1992 there were a total of 426,420 goals in 143,118 games.

ii. How many goals a game is this on average?

a) 2.98
b) 1.22
c) 2.04

In 26,590 games since the Premiership started in 1992, there have been 68,716 goals.

iii. How many goals has that been per game on average?

a) 1.56
b) 2.58
c) 2.09

Answers: i) a ii) a iii) b

Between 1879 and 2005, Kettering Town scored 803 goals in FA Cup competition – the best result of any team.

So if football's about goals, does this mean the game was better in the old days? You decide.

Lots of Pointless Running About

These are the total matches from every World Cup.

	Competition	Number of matches		Competition	Number of matches
1930	Uruguay	18	1974	West Germany	38
1934	Italy	17	1978	Argentina	38
1938	France	18	1982	Spain	52
1950	Brazil	22	1986	Mexico	52
1954	Switzerland	26	1990	Italy	52
1958	Sweden	35	1994	USA	52
1962	Chile	32	1998	France	64
1966	England	32	2002	Korea/Japan	64
1970	Mexico	32			

i. How many World Cup finals games have there been so far?

a) 644
b) 256
c) 419

This averages out at about 38 games a tournament, but in fact, nowadays the World Cup has more finals games than were ever played before the Second World War.

Earlier we learned that each team runs 69.8 miles on average in a Premiership game. Assume this holds true in World Cup games.

Answer: i) a
There have been 124 FA Cup Final games. At 69.8 miles per team per game, this is 17,310 miles or about LA to Sydney the hard way.

ii. Since it began in 1930, how many miles have been run at the World Cup so far?

a) 89,902 miles
b) 133,276 miles
c) 42,003 miles

- *Circumference of the Earth: 24,901 miles*

Switzerland was the Humdinger

These are the total goals from every World Cup.

Competition		Number of goals	Competition		Number of goals
1930	Uruguay	70	1974	West Germany	97
1934	Italy	70	1978	Argentina	102
1938	France	84	1982	Spain	146
1950	Brazil	88	1986	Mexico	132
1954	Switzerland	140	1990	Italy	115
1958	Sweden	126	1994	USA	141
1962	Chile	89	1998	France	171
1966	England	89	2002	Korea/Japan	161
1970	Mexico	95			

i. How many goals have ever been scored at the World Cup finals?

a) 2,238
b) 1,428
c) 1,916

Answers: ii) a i) c

There have been 4 FA Cup trophies: the second, a replica of the first, was last used in 1910 and sold for £420,000 in 2005.

There have been 644 World Cup games so far.

---

ii. Historically, how many goals are scored on average in a World Cup match?

a) 2.98
b) 2.33
c) 1.88

- *Most goals in a single World Cup match: Austria vs. Switzerland 7:5 (1954)*

A Spot of History

The first ever FA Cup Final was played on Saturday, 16 March 1872 at the Kennington Oval. Wanderers, an amateur club who played in London's Battersea Park, beat Royal Engineers 1:0. The single goal was scored by a man named Morton Betts. Little is known about him – save that he played under the pseudonym A.H. Chequer, was an old Harrovian and had played for Harrow Chequers. We also know that when he wasn't playing up front for Wanderers, Betts kept goal for England and played County Cricket for Middlesex and Kent.

Throughout the 1870s, Wanderers won the FA Cup a total of 5 times in 7 years; the last time in 1878. But in 1879, the Cup was won, for their penultimate time, by Old Etonians. They reached the final after beating a team named Darwen in the quarter-final (by a result that demanded two replays). This clash, between Darwen and Old Etonians is particularly remembered because it was the first FA Cup tie that saw 'professionals' take to the pitch: two Scotsmen from Glasgow named Jimmy Love and Fergus Suter.

Answer: i) a
5 wins in the FA Cup puts Wanderers on a par with Everton and West Brom.

(Later, in 1880, Suter, a former stonemason who had played for Partick Thistle and Rangers, would move from Darwen to local rivals Blackburn Rovers, stirring up an ill-tempered atmosphere that would blight future derbies for years after.)

Viewed through the lens of history Darwen, who now play in the North West Counties League, are also remembered for three other things: first for the worst ever defeat in a first division game after they lost 12:0 to West Bromwich Albion during the 1891/92 season. Second, because they are thought to have been the first club to install electric floodlights, and thirdly, and most notably, because in the 1898/99 season they suffered 18 consecutive defeats during their last season in League Division Two.

Assuming (even back then) Darwen players ran a collective 60 miles during an average match ...

> **i. How many miles did Darwen players run in losing matches before their luck changed?**
>
> a) 1,080 miles
> b) 785 miles
> c) 1,426 miles

- *Distance from Manchester to Lisbon: 1,072 miles*

But Why Blackburn Rovers?

The FA Cup competition was very different in the early years, being essentially a social networking system for former public schoolboys, whether gone on to the City, the Army or Oxbridge.

Answer: i) a
The highest score in an FA Cup was in the Matthews Final when Blackpool beat Bolton 4:3 in 1953.

First 12 FA Cup Final results

1872	Wanderers vs. Royal Engineers	1:0
1873	Wanderers vs. Oxford University	2:0
1874	Oxford University vs. Royal Engineers	2:0
1875	Royal Engineers vs. Old Etonians	1:1
	Royal Engineers vs. Old Etonians	2:0
1876	Wanderers vs. Old Etonians	0:0
	Wanderers vs. Old Etonians	3:0
1877	Wanderers vs. Oxford University	2:0 aet
1878	Wanderers vs. Royal Engineers	3:1
1879	Old Etonians vs. Clapham Rovers	1:0
1880	Clapham Rovers vs. Oxford University	1:0
1881	Old Carthusians vs. Old Etonians	3:0
1882	Old Etonians vs. Blackburn Rovers	1:0
1883	Blackburn Olympic vs. Old Etonians	2:1 aet

12 most recent FA Cup Final results

2005*	Arsenal vs. Manchester United	0:0 aet
2004	Manchester United vs. Millwall	3:0
2003	Arsenal vs. Southampton United	1:0
2002	Arsenal vs. Chelsea	2:0
2001	Liverpool vs. Arsenal	2:1
2000	Chelsea vs. Aston Villa	1:0
1999	Manchester United vs. Newcastle United	2:0
1998	Arsenal vs. Newcastle United	2:0
1997	Chelsea vs. Middlesbrough	2:0
1996	Manchester United vs. Liverpool	1:0
1995	Everton vs. Manchester United	1:0
1994	Manchester United vs. Chelsea	4:0

* In 2005, Arsenal ultimately won 5:4 in a penalty shoot-out.

i. How many goals were scored in total during FA Cup Final games during the first 12 years of the competition? (Use aet scores where given.)

a) 22
b) 27
c) 34

The only first-class team to appear in the first dozen FA Cup finals that we would recognise today were Blackburn Rovers who debuted in 1882, the 11th year of the competition. But why Blackburn Rovers? Must be all the aristocrats who live there.

After the game turned professional, teams such as Old Etonians and Royal Engineers were never seen amongst the finalists again. Shame.

ii. How many goals were scored during the last 12 FA Cup Finals?*

a) 19
b) 22
c) 32

(*Use the 0:0 score aet (after extra time) result from the 2005 Arsenal vs. Manchester United confrontation, as games weren't resolved by pso (penalty shoot-out) in the 1870s and 1880s.)

So was the FA Cup more exciting when the Old Etonians were playing? With 2 victories, Old Etonians' FA Cup record matches Sunderland's; it has a better record in the FA Cup Final than 6 current Premiership sides: Portsmouth, Birmingham City, Middlesbrough, Fulham, Charlton Athletic and Wigan Athletic.

Answers: i) b ii) b

Penalty kicks were first introduced in 1891.

The Grit in the Pearl

This is a list of prize money available in 2003/04 at each stage of the English FA Cup.

Stage	Number of winners	Cash each winner received (£)
Winner	1	2,000,000
Runner-up	1	1,000,000
Sixth round proper winners	4	400,000
Fifth round proper winners	8	150,000
Fourth round proper winners	16	75,000
Third round proper winners	32	50,000
Second round proper winners	20	15,000
First round proper winners	40	12,500
Fourth round qualifying winners	32	10,000
Third round qualifying winners	42	5,000
Second round qualifying winners	84	3,750
First round qualifying winners	99	2,250
Preliminary round winners	198	1,000
Extra preliminary winners	65	500

(This means, for example, 65 extra preliminary winners won £500 each.)

Successful teams obviously win money at each successive stage.

i. According to this list, what was the total FA Cup prize money in 2003/04?

a) £12,656,230
b) £10,698,250
c) £9,342,990

Answer: i) b

Until 1961, the maximum a professional footballer could earn in England was £20 a week.

This means that – with a £1,000,000 difference between winner and runner-up – in the 3:0 FA Cup Final that season, Ronaldo cost Millwall £333,333.33 by scoring 1 goal, and van Nistelrooy cost them £666,666.67 with his 2. Do you think Millwall will ever forgive them?

Devilled Herrings

Another lesson from history: Hartlepool United club folklore has it they once bought a player from Workington for a fee of £10 and a box of kippers. At the time of writing, a 5 kg box containing 20 kippers can be bought on the internet for £32. When Manchester United bought Wayne Rooney from Everton in 2004, the deal was allegedly worth £27 million. Imagine Manchester United had paid each and every £42 of the cost as £10 and a box of 20 kippers ...

i. How many kippers would Manchester United have paid for Wayne Rooney?

a) 10,345,981
b) 14,789,002
c) 12,857,143

ii. And how much would all this fish weigh? (A metric tonne is 1,000 kg.)

a) 1,929 tonnes
b) 3,214 tonnes
c) 5,009 tonnes

Answers: i) c ii) b

The first footballer in England to earn £100 a week was former England captain Johnny Haynes in 1961.

- *Fish fried in a British fish-and-chip shop in a month: 4,100 tonnes*
- *Soil beneath old Manchester City Maine Road pitch: 3,000 tonnes*
- *Steel in Blackpool Tower: 2,536 tonnes*
- *Gold mined in a year: 2,500 tonnes*

A shoal of herrings (a kipper is a smoked herring) is loosely described as containing 'hundreds of thousands' of fish. This means Wayne is worth between 14 and 64 shoals. And by the way, that's SHOALS not SCHOLES.

Up Yer Arsenal

The new Wembley Stadium will seat 90,000 people. It will also house 2,618 toilets – reputedly more than any other stadium on Earth.

We all produce about 1 millilitre of urine a minute. The desire to wee can begin when the bladder contains as little as 150 millilitres (though this can usually be resisted until it contains 4 or 5 times more). This means we get the urge to pee about every $2\frac{1}{2}$ hours.

So one day, off you go to the shiny new Wembley stadium at, er, Wembley. Let's be honest, you aren't going to get in, watch a match including stoppages, and get out again in much under, say, $2\frac{1}{2}$ hours.

So we can safely assume that, on average, every spectator at Wembley will get the urge to pee once at any given fixture.

(We'll forget the potential problems: the rush at half-time; the broken and blocked loos; the soiled and inaccessible; the 'sorry mate, the only free cubicle at the moment is half a kilometre around the other side'; and, of course, the curse of four pints before the match ...)

i. On average how many people will visit each Wembley toilet at a single fixture?

a) 102
b) 34
c) 85

Assume it takes 2.5 hours to enjoy a fixture at Wembley.

ii. On average, how often will each toilet at Wembley get used?

a) Every 1.51 minutes
b) Every 4.36 minutes
c) Every 9.12 minutes

You can already bet there'll be queues. Just hope there aren't too many number twos ...

How Do You Spell In-ger-land! in British Sign Language?

I really do mean it, how do you spell *In-ger-land!* in British Sign Language? Answers to www.footballfreaking.co.uk please.

Answers: i) b ii) b

The volume of water flowing over Niagara Falls could fill the new Wembley in 11 minutes 7 seconds.

These are the results from every football Final from the World Games for the Deaf.

1924	France vs. Great Britain	2:0	1969	Yugoslavia vs. Russia	1:1
1928	Great Britain vs. Czechoslovakia	2:1	1973	Russia vs. Sweden	4:1
1931	Germany vs. Austria	4:1	1977	Romania vs. Russia	4:0
1935	Great Britain vs. Belgium	4:2	1981	Russia vs. Hungary	4:1
1939	Great Britain vs. Sweden	2:1	1985	Italy vs. Great Britain	2:1
1949	Great Britain vs. Belgium	6:4	1989	Great Britain vs. Ireland	5:0
1953	Yugoslavia vs. Italy	2:1	1993	Greece vs. Czechoslovakia	2:1
1957	Yugoslavia vs. Italy	6:0	1997	Turkey vs. France	3:1
1961	Yugoslavia vs. Belgium	4:1	2001	Italy vs. Germany	2:0
1965	Yugoslavia vs. Great Britain	3:1	2005	Great Britain vs. Iran	2:1

i. On average, how many goals have been scored at each football Final at the 20 World Games for the Deaf?

a) 4.15
b) 3.55
c) 2.95

ii. Which score below is closest to the average score for a World Games for the Deaf Final?

a) 2:2
b) 2:1
c) 3:1

In terms of goals then, the competition's as exciting as the average World Cup Final. You'll notice the Great Britain team has won 6 times since its inception: something all Britain's international teams might do well to note.

(Well done lads.)

Answers: i) a ii) c

Argentina's 19 July 1930 win over Mexico saw Guillermo Stabile score the first ever World Cup hat-trick.

Tor!

Now obviously if you've got the World Cup in your own country, you'd want to see your team play.

Though they may well play more matches, Germany are only guaranteed 3 appearances at their World Cup. These are their group stage matches in Munich, Dortmund and Berlin.

	Stadium	Seating capacity
Berlin	Olympiastadion	74,500
Dortmund	FIFA World Cup Stadium	67,000
Munich	FIFA World Cup Stadium	66,000

And how many fans will vie for these seats? The German Soccer Federation (DFB) has 6,272,803 members. We'll assume none of them would turn down a ticket. Plus, the German authorities anticipate 1 million fans from abroad in-country during the competition. So even ignoring the other 75 million Germans who might like to catch a Germany game, we'll assume at least 7,272,803 people in Germany during the finals would like to see a Germany match.

i. On these numbers, how many people will compete for each ticket to see Germany play?

a) 23
b) 48
c) 35

• *Overall, there's the equivalent of 1 ticket to see Germany play for every 397 Germans.*

Do you think tournament supremo Franz Beckenbauer would get you one?

Answer: i) c

German police were monitoring 6,800 known hooligans in the run-up to the 2006 World Cup.

Us and Them

In England, people tend to refer to the national team in terms of 'us' or 'we', while in France, they tend to characterize their team in terms of 'them' and 'they'. Perhaps it says something about obsession ...

According to a study in the North of England, the number of men who die from heart attacks increases by 28% when the local professional football team lose.

- *While these findings could be replicated in Holland, they couldn't in France*

In Britain, around 125,000 men suffer a heart attack every year. Of these, about 34,000 effectively 'drop dead' (as opposed to surviving or dying later). Though the number and severity of heart attacks varies from day to day, for example, attacks are more likely to be fatal in the winter), on average about 93 men drop dead from heart attacks every day. Assume about 90% of them (83) are English.

Presumably, therefore, if England are knocked out of the World Cup, 28% more men will drop dead than would have done otherwise.

i. So how many men might die of a heart attack if England lose?
a) 33
b) 23
c) 13

Or 1 for every player in the England squad ...

According to the doctors who did the original study, this increased risk of a heart attack can be counteracted by taking a couple of aspirin daily – apparently – but it's up to you to double check.

Answer: i) b

Cardiovascular disease (CVD) kills about 238,000 people a year in the UK.

Lucky to Get Nil ...

Poor Scotland. When they played Estonia in a World Cup qualifier in 1996, FIFA said the match should start 3 hours early because of rubbish floodlights, Estonia refused to even turn up ... and Scotland still didn't win. The game kicked off. The referee blew his whistle to end the fiasco. FIFA ordered the match to be replayed ... and the Scots were held 0:0 in Monaco.

It was ever thus. At the first ever Scotland vs. England International, at Hamilton Crescent Glasgow on 30 November 1872, Scotland went on in the latest 2-2-6 formation, expecting to outplay England in their traditional 1-1-8, but the match ended in a nil-nil draw too.

But the Scottish team must have felt optimistic when, finally, a little over 3 months later on 8 March 1873, they took England on again at Kennington Oval in London ... ever plucky, they lost 4:2.

Social scientists define 'a generation' as 30 years. Here are the results from every England vs. Scotland game in the last 30 years ...

Date	England vs. Scotland	Date	England vs. Scotland
17.11.99	0:1	26.05.84	1:1
13.11.99	2:0	01.06.83	2:0
15.06.96	2:0	29.05.82	1:0
27.05.89	2:0	23.05.81	0:1
21.05.88	1:0	24.05.80	2:0
23.05.87	0:0	26.05.79	3:1
23.04.86	2:1	21.05.78	1:0
25.05.85	0:1	04.06.77	1:2

In all this time, Scotland have only ever managed 2 goals against England once.

i. How many goals have England scored against Scotland for every 2 goals scored by Scotland since 1977?

a) 1
b) 5
c) 3

Yet every time they play the English, Scotland think they might win ...

'I haven't felt that good since Archie Gemmill scored against Holland in 1978.'

Renton in the movie *Trainspotting*.

Here at *Football Freaking*, we follow a simple formula: the more goals, the more exciting the football. There may be exceptions occasionally, but basically it's as easy as that ...

These are the scoring records of the top 8 goal scorers in both the English and Scottish Premier Leagues at the end of the 2004/05 season.

English Premiership			
Player	Club	Goals	Matches
Thierry Henry	Arsenal	25	31
Andrew Johnson	Crystal Palace	21	37
Robert Pires	Arsenal	14	26
Jermain Defoe	Tottenham	13	28
Aiyegbeni Yakubu	Portsmouth	13	29
Andy Cole	Fulham	12	29
Jimmy Hasselbaink	Middlesbrough	13	36
Frank Lampard	Chelsea	13	38

Answer: i) b

Scotland's worst defeat was a 7:0 stomping by Uruguay in Switzerland at the 1954 World Cup.

| Scottish Premier League | | | |
Player	Club	Goals	Matches
John Hartson	Celtic	25	38
Derek Riordan	Hibernian	20	36
Nacho Novo	Rangers	19	33
Dado Prso	Rangers	18	33
Kris Boyd	Kilmarnock	17	29
Scott McDonald	Motherwell	15	26
Chris Sutton	Celtic	12	25
Garry O'Connor	Hibernian	14	34

For both English and Scottish scorers the cumulative game total is 254.

i. How many goals did these players from the English Premiership score between them?

a) 124
b) 173
c) 89

ii. How many goals did these players from the Scottish Premier League score between them?

a) 140
b) 76
c) 129

Which suggests the reports that English football can be the most boring in the world might be correct.

Maybe we really should give thanks for Scottish goalies.

Answers: i) a ii) a

Scotland's biggest win came in 1878 in a 9:0 victory over Wales (their worst ever defeat).

Watch With Mutter

Here's a list of the total number of spectators who've attended the 17 World Cups.

Year	Host	Total spectators
1930	Uruguay	434,000
1934	Italy	395,000
1938	France	483,000
1950	Brazil	1,337,000
1954	Switzerland	943,000
1958	Sweden	868,000
1962	Chile	776,000
1966	England	1,614,677
1970	Mexico	1,673,975
1974	West Germany	1,774,022
1978	Argentina	1,610,215
1982	Spain	1,856,277
1986	Mexico	2,407,431
1990	Italy	2,517,348
1994	USA	3,587,538
1998	France	2,785,100
2002	Korea/Japan	2,722,390

i. How many fans have ever attended a World Cup match?

a) 18,223,903
b) 27,784,973
c) 37,675,223

Answer: i) b

Scotland have qualified for the World Cup 8 times.

- *Population of Syria: 18,448,752*
- *Population of Peru: 27,925,628*
- *Population of Poland: 38,557,984*

There are 3 countries that have already hosted the World Cup twice: Italy, where a total of 2,912,348 spectators (about the current population of Wales) have ever watched a World Cup finals game and Mexico, where a total of 4,081,406 spectators (about the current population of Ireland) have ever watched one. The third is France, where 3,268,100 fans (about the population of late-14th-century England) caught a game. After the 2006 World Cup, Germany will join the World-Cup-host-twice-over club. With a total of about 3.45 million seats available in 2006, the total number of spectators after-wards who will ever have watched a World Cup match in Germany will be about the population of modern Scotland.

Lost

The Jules Rimet trophy, the first World Cup, was cast by a French sculptor named Abel Lafleur in the shape of a goblet borne by Nike (the ancient Greek goddess of victory) from 3.8 kg of pure gold. In 1970 in Mexico City, it was won in perpetuity by Brazil, when they became the first country to win it 3 times.

But then someone forgot to lock a window (or something), because it was stolen in Rio in 1983 and never recovered. Rumour is it was melted down.

At the time of writing, the London spot price for gold is £270.10 per troy ounce.

A troy ounce is about 31.1 grams.

> **i. About how much is a 3.8 kg, solid-gold trophy worth at the current gold spot price?**
>
> a) £65,000
> b) £33,000
> c) £16,000

- *Annual retainer the FA pays to Britain's top 21 referees: £33,000 each*

None of which explains why the Greeks named a goddess after a sports shoe.

Bogarding the Joint

After joining Chelsea on a free transfer from Barcelona, Dutch defender Winston Bogarde was paid a basic salary of £40,000 a week for the next 4 years – a total of £8,320,000 during his 'career' at Stamford Bridge. Yet he made only 12 appearances; the equivalent of £693,000 per run out.

Teams in the English Premiership play a basic 38 games a season excluding Cup games.

> **i. At £693,000 for each of 38 games, how much would this be?**
>
> a) £26,334,000
> b) £19,776,000
> c) £38,229,000

Which is almost twice the combined basic annual salary of £4.4 million that Real Madrid reputedly pays to Beckham, Ronaldo and Zidane.

- *Reported approximate basic annual salary of Beckham, Ronaldo and Zidane combined: £13.2 million*

Answers: i) b i) a

An official replica of the Jules Rimet trophy was sold at auction in 1997 for £254,500.

Toeing the Line

One of the best-paid players in the world is reputed to be Chelsea midfielder Frank Lampard – who reportedly earns a basic annual salary of £5.2 million a year or £100,000 a week.

The Chelsea pitch measures 113 x 74 yards. Human walking speed is said to average 4 feet a second.

i. Based on his weekly salary, how much does Frank earn in the time it would take to walk around the Chelsea pitch?

a) £70.33
b) £46.37
c) £28.90

It's said that if Bill Gates' fortune stopped growing for the 4 seconds it might take him to pick a $100 bill off the floor, he'd be worse off than if he just left it.

So imagine if, as he walked around the Chelsea pitch, Frank spotted a €1 coin. (Perhaps dropped earlier by Jose Mourinho pacing the sideline.)

ii. About how much would he earn during the 4 seconds he took to pick it up?

a) £1.00
b) €1.00 (£0.67)
c) US $1.00 (£0.56)

(Admittedly, Frank can probably pick things off the floor in considerably less than 4 seconds.)

Answers: i) b ii) b

Currently Bill Gates is worth $27.94 billion. Manchester United cost the Glazers £790 million; Bill could buy MU 19 times over.

Being Frank

So if you happen to find a Frank Lampard in your team, what kind of performance can you expect? In the season 2004/05 (the last complete season at the time of writing) Frank scored a total of 23 goals. On the international front, he scored 4 playing for England (including 1 in extra time) and 4 playing for Chelsea in the Champions League. On the domestic front, Frank scored 2 playing for Chelsea in the Carling Cup and 13 playing for Chelsea in the Premiership (including 3 penalties).

These are the games in which Frank Lampard scored in 2004/05

Date	Fixture	Score at full-time	Lampard goals	Time elapsed (minutes)
Friendly				
05.06.04	England vs. Iceland	6:1	1	25
European Championship				
13.06.04	France vs. England	2:1	1	38
21.06.04	Croatia vs. England	2:4	1	79
24.06.04	Portugal vs. England	2:2	1	115
Carling Cup				
30.11.04	Fulham vs. Chelsea	1:2	1	88
26.01.05	Manchester United vs. Chelsea	1:2	1	29
Champions League				
08.03.05	Chelsea vs. Barcelona	4:2	1	17
06.04.05	Chelsea vs. Bayern München	4:2	2	60, 70
12.04.05	Bayern München vs. Chelsea	3:2	1	30
Premiership				
28.08.04	Chelsea vs. Southampton	2:1	1	46 (pen)
30.10.04	West Bromwich Albion vs. Chelsea	1:4	1	81
13.11.04	Fulham vs. Chelsea	1:4	1	33
04.12.04	Chelsea vs. Newcastle	4:0	1	63
18.12.04	Chelsea vs. Norwich	4:0	1	34
15.01.05	Tottenham Hotspur vs. Chelsea	0:2	2	39 (pen), 90
19.03.05	Chelsea vs. Crystal Palace	4:1	1	29
02.04.05	Southampton vs. Chelsea	1:3	1	22
23.04.05	Chelsea vs. Fulham	3:1	1	64
30.04.05	Bolton vs. Chelsea	0:2	2	60, 76
15.05.05	Newcastle vs. Chelsea	1:1	1	35 (pen)

For the purpose of these Football Freaks, ignore the penalties and the goal Frank scored against Portugal after 115 minutes.

> **i. When Frank scored in the first half, how many minutes did he take to score on average?**
>
> a) 18.5
> b) 28.6
> c) 38.5

> **ii. Including every time Frank scored in the second half, how many minutes did he take to score on average?**
>
> a) 60.5
> b) 66.5
> c) 73.1

This spread of goals would seem to suggest defenders can relax for the first quarter-hour of each half. But this season Frank has upped his game. So far in 2005/06 (at the time of writing), he has scored 11 times including 2 penalties. Never yet in the first 15 minutes of the first half, but 3 times in the first 15 of the second. Football Freaking? We love it!

Slash, Unnecessary Detail

There are some issues that perplex football - homophobia, crowd violence and racism for example - about which *Football Freaking* can offer little if anything new. Clubs, supporters and authorities have united firmly against violence and racism and *Football Freaking* applauds them. Roma fans may

Answers: i) b ii) b

Evolution in action: Frank Lampard (senior), 2 England caps; Frank Lampard (junior), 38 England caps.

display Nazi symbols (and be slung in jail for it, hopefully), but this isn't something that still happens every week in Britain.

The issue of homophobia in football is altogether more recent, at least in terms of its presence in the public domain. And so what can *Football Freaking* tell you that you may not find elsewhere?

Surveys suggest 15% of people in Britain have had a same-sex experience. This suggests such an experience has been enjoyed by ...

---

i. How many players among England's 23-strong playing squad?

a) 4
b) 9
c) 14

---

ii. How many players among the 437 squad members in England's Premiership league?

a) 66
b) 32
c) 135

Premium Priced

When Sir Alex Ferguson was negotiating with German captain and Bayern München midfielder Michael Ballack to come to Old Trafford, the Manchester United manager allegedly put a deal rumoured to be worth £6 million on the table.

Answers: i) a ii) a

Bayern München's sponsorship deal with T-Com is reputedly worth £11.6 million: over £1 million per man on-pitch.

> **i. Michael weighs 80 kg. How much is that a gram?**
>
> a) £75
> b) £55
> c) £35

Father-of-three Michael has been voted Germany's most handsome footballer by readers of several German women's magazines. Presumably by women who'd pay considerably more to keep him in Germany if they could!

- *Street price of cocaine: £40 a gram*

Blame It On Rio

With a salary package reportedly worth £5.5 million a year, presumably Rio Ferdinand smiles a lot. Dentists advise that good dental hygiene requires 2 minutes correct brushing twice a day.

> **i. Provided he remembers, how much does Rio Ferdinand earn in the 4 minutes he should spend brushing his teeth every day?**
>
> a) £61.76
> b) £51.56
> c) £41.86

Technically there are 32 teeth in a full adult set. So that's £1.31 a tooth ...

But a bit more in Rio's case.

Who Ate the Pies? You Did.

Echelon	Attendance 2004/05
Premiership	12,879,441
Championship	9,588,921
League One	4,271,104
League Two	2,479,744
Nationwide conference	887,674
Total	30,106,884

A 250 g supermarket steak pie contains 36% beef.

8% of Britons claim they are vegetarian. Why should football fans be different? Imagine 8% of football fans are vegetarians too.

Imagine every carnivorous fan who attended a Premiership game ate a 250 g steak pie at every match they attended.

i. How many metric tonnes (1,000 kg) of beef would Premiership fans consume over the season?

a) 1,066.4
b) 652.9
c) 2,331.7

A beef carcass yields about 140 kg of edible meat.

ii. How many cattle would it take to make this many pies?

a) 4,345
b) 7,618
c) 12,456

Answers: i) a ii) b

When William Henry 'Fatty' Foulke transferred from Sheffield United to Chelsea, the transfer fee was £50.

The average UK beef cattle herd has about 26 animals. So in a season, fans could theoretically consume about 293 herds of cattle in pies ...

The chant 'Who ate all the pies?' is said to allude to a goalie named William Foulke, who briefly played for Chelsea a century ago during the 1905/06 season. Famous for his 22½ stone (140 kg) bulk, Mr Foulke was also noted for his agility. Once, when there was some dispute over club colours, legend has it he was obliged to wrap a white sheet around himself. When the sheet finished the game as clean as it started, it spawned the term 'clean sheet'.

Football Matches Available Here

In preparation for the 2002 World Cup, South Korea spent US $2.7 billion (€2.26 billion) on infrastructure, and Japan spent $4.6 billion (€3.85 billion). Indeed, the Korean city of Daegu reportedly spent its total annual budget to build Korea's biggest World Cup stadium – even though the city had no football club ...

Similarly in Germany, supported by federal grants, the cities chosen to host the games have dug deep into their pockets to build, replace or restore stadiums fit for *der Fussball-Weltmeisterschaft Deutschland 2006.*

Here is a list of cities and stadiums, the investment made in each and the number of stadium seats each has or will make available to spectators' nethers.

Real Madrid's sponsorship deal with BenQ is reputedly worth £13.5 million a year.

City	Population (millions)	Stadium	Investment (€ million)	Number of seats
Berlin	3.39	Olympiastadion	242	74,500
Cologne	1.02	Rhein Energie Stadion*	110	45,000
Dortmund	0.59	Westfalenstadion*	34	67,000
Frankfurt	0.65	Waldstadion*	126	48,000
Gelsenkirchen	0.28	Arena Auf Schalke*	192	51,000
Hamburg	1.70	AOL Arena*	97	50,000
Hanover	0.53	AWD Arena*	63	45,000
Kaiserslautern	0.10	Fritz-Walter-Stadion	48.3	48,500
Leipzig	0.50	Zentralstadion	90.6	42,655
Munich	1.30	Allianz Arena*	280	66,000
Nuremberg	0.50	Franken-Stadion	56	45,500
Stuttgart	0.59	Gottlieb-Daimler-Stadion	51.5	54,500

* Due to FIFA rules prohibiting the use of stadium sponsors' names during the World Cup finals, the stadium names marked will be known, for the duration, by the name 'FIFA World Cup Stadium ...' followed by the location: Cologne, Hamburg, Hanover, etc.

So as a hypothetical spectator, touring these stadiums ...

i. Which city spent the most on your seat?

a) Munich
b) Berlin
c) Cologne

ii. Which city apparently spent the most per citizen on seating your bottom?

a) Kaiserslautern
b) Gelsenkirchen
c) Frankfurt

Answers: i) a ii) b

35,000 German police officers have had their leave cancelled due to the 2006 World Cup and they ain't happy.

In fact, much of the money invested in German World Cup football stadiums came from federal grants and/or private sources.

So Many Jokes, So Many Sneers

This is a list of football singles you've probably never heard of. Cast your mind back, do none of them ring a bell? Didn't think so.

Teams

Arsenal FC	Hot Stuff	1998
Aston Villa FC	We're Going Up	1975
Brighton & Hove Albion FC	The Old Brighton Blue	1983
Celtic FC	Celtic Your Favourites in Green	1973
Chelsea FC	No One Can Stop Us Now	1994
Crystal Palace FC	Glad All Over	1990
Glasgow Rangers FC	Nine in a Row	1997
Liverpool FC	Sitting on Top of the World	1986
Manchester Utd FC	United (We Love You)	1993
Middlesbrough FC (and Chris Rea)	Let's Dance	1997
Newcastle United (written by Sting)	Black & White Army	1998
Nottingham Forest (with Paper Lace)	We've Got the Whole World in Our Hands	1978
Tottenham Hotspur FC	Tottenham Tottenham	1982
West Ham United FC	I'm Forever Blowing Bubbles	1975

Players

Gazza (Paul Gascoigne)	Geordie Boys	1990
Glen Hoddle and Chris Waddle	Diamond Lights	1987
Peter Shilton and Ray Clemence	Side By Side	1980
Kevin Keegan	Head Over Heels in Love	1979

National sides

Northern Ireland Football Team	Come On Northern Ireland	1986
Republic Of Ireland Squad	The Boys in Green	1988
Scottish World Cup Squad	Say it with Pride	1990
England Football Squad	We've Got the Whole World at Our Feet	1986

***Football Freaking*'s all-time favourite**

Albanian Football Squad	Albania! Albania!	1982

It almost certainly won't surprise you to know that the most successful football single of all time was 'Three Lions' by David Baddiel and Frank Skinner and The Lightning Seeds, which originally spent 15 weeks in the chart, including 2 weeks at number 1, in the summer of 1996. It was then re-released in 1998, when it spent 13 weeks in the chart, including 3 weeks at number 1.

So successful was this tune that the German team, fresh from knocking England out in the semi-finals at Euro 96, reputedly sang it in their team coach on their way to their Wembley final. (They won 2:1 aet against the Czech Republic.)

No reliable data is available on the number of sales 'Three Lions' notched up: but we do know it went platinum, which nowadays translates into sales of 600,000 copies. The total number of spectators who attended Euro 96, meanwhile, was 1,317,381. The total attendance at England's games at Euro 96 was 381,531.

> **i. How many spectators attended a Euro 96 game for every copy sold of 'Three Lions'?**
>
> a) 1.6
> b) 3.0
> c) 2.2

No doubt 'Three Lions' will one day be re-mixed and re-released. The Football Freaking Forecast is for sooner rather than later; it sells too well not to.

Answer: i) c

A Manchester United team-shirt autographed by 11 first-team players from the 2003/04 season costs £350.

Football's Coming Home

After Brazil won the Jules Rimet trophy outright, the replacement cup – officially known as the FIFA World Cup – was first up for grabs in the 1974 final, when it was won by West Germany *in* West Germany (when they beat Holland 2:1).

So if Germany win this time (and you always have to fancy the home side), the FIFA World Cup might well be coming home and there's nothing the three lions can do about it.

The FIFA World Cup, depicting 2 athletes supporting the world, was cast by a Milanese artist named Silvio Gazzaniga. Now available strictly on a 4-year loan-only basis, the FIFA World Cup stands 36 centimetres tall atop a malachite base, and now contains 4.97 kg, but this time of only 18-carat (just 75%) gold.

The price of gold is £270.10 per troy ounce. A troy ounce is about 31.1 grams.

> ### i. About how much is the FIFA World Cup worth at the current gold price?
>
> a) £3,237
> b) £323,729
> c) £32,372

The FIFA World Cup has already been home for the holidays once before – after Germany (managed by Franz Beckenbauer) beat Argentina 1:0 at the final in Rome in 1990.

Answer: i) c

The name plaques on the FIFA World Cup base will all be filled after the 2038 World Cup.

Tout Heaven

Whatever happens, someone will have to make money at Germany 2006 ...

City	Stadium	Number of seats	Number of matches
Berlin	Olympiastadion	74,500	6
Cologne (Koln)	FIFA World Cup Stadium	45,000	5
Dortmund	FIFA World Cup Stadium	67,000	6
Frankfurt am Main	FIFA World Cup Stadium	48,000	5
Gelsenkirchen	FIFA World Cup Stadium	51,000	5
Hamburg	FIFA World Cup Stadium	50,000	5
Hanover	FIFA World Cup Stadium	45,000	5
Kaiserslautern	Fritz-Walter-Stadion	48,500	5
Leipzig	Zentralstadion	42,655	5
Munich	FIFA World Cup Stadium	66,000	6
Nuremberg	Franken-Stadion	45,500	5
Stuttgart	Gottlieb-Daimler-Stadion	54,500	6

(For argument's sake, assume the same number of seats are available for all games at each venue.)

i. How many seats are available for the entire competition?

a) 3,450,275
b) 345,053
c) 34,505

Assume demand gives each ticket an average potential black-market value of €500.

Answer: i) a

England group tickets average €843 (£570) from a web agency. World Cup Final tickets are at least €2,250 (£1,522).

ii. What would be the potential 'black-market' value of all the spectator tickets to the World Cup combined?

a) €2,331,567,200
b) €1,725,137,500
c) €634,453,000

Which, be fair, is enough to get you interested ...

Sorry, Which One is the Religion Again?

At Germany 2006 there'll be a chronic lack of stadium seats. Germany's Evangelical Church will help by showing the 2006 World Cup matches free of charge, meaning up to 16,000 churches and parish halls will play their own special part in the football extravaganza.

Assume every church and parish hall will hold 200 people each on average.

i. How many extra seats could this all create for each match?

a) 3,200,000
b) 1,100,000
c) 5,200,000

Lucky fans ...

In fact, Pope Benedict XVI was criticised in some parts for bestowing his blessing on the 2006 tournament. Unlike the previous pope, who took an enthusiastic interest in the game, Benedict XVI had shown little interest in it.

Answers: ii) b i) a

The first televised World Cup finals were held in Switzerland in 1954.

As to whether the blessing might give the German team an unfair advantage, a spokesman for the German organising committee said: 'The Pope is a Bavarian. Franz Beckenbauer (head of the competition's organising committee) is a Bavarian. They know each other.'

Warming Up

Preliminary games for the 2006 World Cup:

Region	Matches	Goals	Crowd
African Zone	190	506	4,995,187
Asian Zone	135	401	2,856,858
European Zone	282	778	5,825,195
North, Central American and Caribbean Zone	111	379	1,642,995
Oceanian Zone	38	164	266,356
South American Zone	91	236	3,071,252
Total	847	2,464	18,657,843

During these preliminary games ...

i. What was the average crowd in the African Zone?

a) 42,004
b) 31,337
c) 26,290

ii. What was the average crowd in the Asian Zone?

a) 28,331
b) 21,162
c) 19,232

Answers: i) c ii) b

Goal nets were first used in 1890.

iii. What was the average crowd in the European Zone?

a) 18,204
b) 20,657
c) 10,465

iv. What was the average crowd in the North, Central American and Caribbean Zone?

a) 16,364
b) 12,446
c) 14,802

v. What was the average crowd in the Oceanian Zone?

a) 7,009
b) 6,213
c) 9,483

vi. What was the average crowd in the South American Zone?

a) 33,750
b) 35,512
c) 35,775

vii. What was the average crowd worldwide?

a) 20,234
b) 24,546
c) 22,028

Answers: iii) b iv) c v) a vi) a vii) c

The biggest football stadium on Earth is the Estadio Azteca in Mexico City, which holds 114,600 fans.

- *Average crowd West Ham game 2005/06: 33,667*
- *Average crowd Charlton Athletic game 2005/06: 26,130*
- *Average crowd Wigan game 2005/06: 20,725*
- *Average crowd Swansea game 2005/06: 14,631*
- *Average crowd Yeovil game 2005/06: 7,111*

Impossible Odds

A total of 3,450,275 seats will technically be available for the 2006 World Cup. But 440,000 of these tickets – more than 1 in 8 – will be reserved for VIPs and the media, leaving about 3 million for fans.

Indeed, for the Final in Berlin on Sunday 9 July, over a quarter of tickets have already been withdrawn from public sale, leaving just 55,562 available for fans. So on average how many football fans will vie for each of these seats? Surely everyone on Earth would like to see a World Cup Final?

Whatever the answer, it's impossible to know before the online sale begins ... which isn't an answer we can really work with at *Football Freaking*. However, earlier we assumed that at least 7,272,803 people will chase tickets to watch Germany: a million visiting overseas fans and the 6,272,803 members of the German Soccer Federation (DFB).

We'll work with these numbers again here.

i. At least how many fans will chase each ticket available for the Final?

a) 65
b) 96
c) 130

Answer: i) c

On average, the winning score in the World Cup Final is about 3:1.

That would be about 113 German Soccer Federation (DFB) members and 18 overseas fans after each and every one.

A 1 in 130 chance isn't that remote. For, example it's about the chance you'll experience a minor assault this year. But it's also about the chance you'll correctly predict the toss of a coin 7 times in a row. Give it a whirl. How did you get on?

Multi-National?

It doesn't matter how many countries are represented at the World Cup – most of the world's top players play in Europe. In Korea/Japan 2002, 351 players represented 32 countries.

Club location	2002 World Cup players		Population (millions)	
Europe	264	(75.2%)	727	(11.4%)
Africa (and Middle East)	19	(5.4%)	877.5	(13.7%)
Asia (mainly China)	26	(7.4%)	3,879	(60.6%)
The Americas	42	(12.0%)	881	(13.8%)
Oceania	0	(0.0%)	32	(0.5%)
Total	351		6,396.5	(global 2005/06)

So when aliens invade planet Earth and challenge humankind to a footballing-duel-to-the-death, which we have to win or they'll zap us with a special ray gun thingy ... (film rights to this idea are available via the author's agent) ... And the aliens say we have to have a team that numerically represents all the different continents in proportion to their populations – because really the aliens are good aliens who want us to live together in peace and solve global warming and stuff ... then the team – we'll call it Earth United – should include 727 divided by 6,396.5 x 11 = $1^{1}/_{4}$ Europeans ...

i. Approximately how many Africans should play for Earth United?

a) $1\frac{1}{2}$
b) $2\frac{3}{4}$
c) $3\frac{1}{2}$

ii. Approximately how many Asians?

a) $4\frac{1}{2}$
b) $3\frac{3}{4}$
c) $6\frac{2}{3}$

iii. Approximately how many Americans?

a) $2\frac{3}{4}$
b) $1\frac{1}{2}$
c) $1\frac{1}{4}$

Team numbers might be made up by one-twelfth of an Oceanian.

Obviously some secret United Nations agency would have to do the special surgery to make half an African or a quarter of a European or whatever, or to save time Earth United could just have 6 players from Asia, 1 each from Europe, Africa and the Americas; and 2 members with more cosmopolitan roots. You decide.

But the key question is, if you were casting a movie of this idea, do you think Frank Lampard and Pelé would both do cameos? And would you choose Halle Berry or Angelina Jolie to run on in the last 3 minutes to save the match? *Football Freaking* is thinking Halle ... but Angelina if it gets us Brad in the Sven role.

Answers: i) a ii) c iii) b

Franz Beckenbauer has 1 credit as a movie actor; in the 1967 comic film *Die Spaßvögel* (The Fun Birds).

England Vs. Paraguay

We'll now consider England's group-stage clash with Paraguay in Frankfurt at the 2006 World Cup. Now at the risk of sounding repetitive: this book was published a full week before the 2006 World Cup kicked off. But still, *Football Freaking* is prepared to make cast-iron, copper-bottomed confident predictions for every result in the competition ... So here it is: England will crush Paraguay like an insignificant insect, then grind up its bones and eat them for its tea. No, not that ... (sorry this book seems to have been momentarily possessed by a fairytale ogre) ... what we meant to say was – despite England's superior Football Freaking Factor:

	FIFA Rank	Population	Per capita GDP	3F
England	9	50,598,940	24,700	0.27
Paraguay	30	6,347,884	4,005	6.66

And despite England's superior match history: 2 previous games; 2 England victories; an aggregate score 7:0 to England ...

... England's recent form: an aggregate of 13:4 in their last 6 internationals ...

and that the Paraguayan team were runners-up in the 2004 Olympics, and that Rubén Darío Aguilera scored 20 times in 18 games in 2005 ...

After weighing up all these factors, *Football Freaking* forecasts a sloppy 1:1 draw.

The venue – the all-new, 48,000-seat, €126-million stadium – is built on the site of the old Waldstadion erected in the 1920s; warmly remembered for games like the water-logged 1974 World Cup semi-final, when West Germany beat Poland 1:0 ... Oh, how we laughed! ...

Frankfurt am Main (to use the city's full German name) is known locally by its population of 650,000 as Mainhattan (ah, bless) after its skyscrapers and financial district.

The population of Manhattan (USA) is 1,537,195.

> **i. About how many people live in Manhattan for every one who lives in Mainhattan?**
>
> a) 0.556
> b) 1.765
> c) 2.365

Frankfurt was also, by the by, the birthplace of Germany's greatest poet, Johann Wolfgang von Goethe (1749-1832), who when asked about Number Freaking said: 'Mathematicians are like Frenchmen: whatever you say to them they translate into their own language and forthwith it is something entirely different.'

Virtual Football

Every day during the 30-day 2002 World Cup in Japan and South Korea, there were 3 times more hits on the fifaworldcup.com website than there were on the official website for the 1998 World Cup in France during the entire tournament.

In 2002, the website received 1.75 billion hits over 30 days.

> **i. How many hits did the website receive each day?**
>
> a) 58.3 million
> b) 42.9 million
> c) 77.0 million

Answers: i) c i) a

Football joined the Olympics in 1900 and Upton Park FC won the Gold. At the first try to include the game in 1896, no teams turned up.

Which works out at 675 hits a second, 24/7.

So it's of comparative interest that when the official ticket server for the 2006 World Cup opened for business, it got 9,000 hits a second and was still getting 1,500 a second, 24 hours later. Later still, when the second phase of ticket sales opened, it took about an hour to sell out team-specific tickets for countries comprising about 5% of the global population: Australia, Costa Rica, Côte d'Ivoire and Croatia went, so did Czech Republic, Ecuador, Iran, Paraguay and Poland too. Saudi Arabia, Serbia and Montenegro, South Korea, Switzerland and Ukraine all went as well. And if you haven't got a net connection? Or you have a bad one? Bad luck ...

The Bit They Never Mention ...

FIFA has said the total prize money at the 2006 World Cup will be 332 million Swiss francs (CHF), the equivalent of £145.8 million.

Though of course it won't, imagine this money was divided between the 352 players representing their countries at Germany 2006.

Under these terms ...

i. How much would each player receive?

a) £266,615
b) £414,205
c) £751,589

Would Franz Beckenbauer give each of the players a personal cheque?

Answer: i) b

The Football Foundation charity backs 1,897 projects with £360 million: www.footballfoundation.org.uk.

In fact, FIFA will provide each of the 32 teams in the World Cup with 1 million CHF in advance and 2 million CHF for every game they play in the groups round – a guarantee of 7 million CHF (£3.1 million) each. The 8 losers in the second round (the round of 16) will each receive a further 1.5 million CHF, and the 4 losers at the quarter-finals an additional 4.5 million CHF each. The winner will receive an extra 17.5 million CHF, the runner-up another 15.5 million CHF and the 2 losing semi-finalists 14.5 million CHF more each. FIFA has a 15 million CHF insurance fund put aside to cover player injuries during the tournament, and will bear some of the travel and accommodation costs for up to 45 people accredited to each of the 32 delegations.

Not Enough

At the 2006 World Cup, under the team-specific ticket system, each country will be guaranteed 8% of the tickets for the matches their teams play. In other words, about 1 in 13 tickets at each England game will be pre-allocated to England fans.

Here are the details of England's guaranteed games during the group stage.

Date	Opponent	Location	Stadium seating
10.6.06	Paraguay	Frankfurt	48,000
15.6.06	Trinidad and Tobago	Nuremberg	45,500
20.6.06	Sweden	Cologne	45,000

i. What is the total number of tickets guaranteed to England fans?

a) 34,000
b) 68,030
c) 11,080

Answer: i) c

A reported 22,446 Socceroo fans scrambled for the 8,500 tickets awarded to Australia.

So if there are 100,000 England fans afoot in Germany, how many England fans will be competing for each guaranteed England ticket?

> **ii. What is the total number of England fans competing for each guaranteed England ticket?**
>
> a) 3
> b) 2
> c) 9

The Question of Sven

When we come to consider the scheduled World Cup groups game confrontation in Cologne between England and Sweden on 20 June 2006, we could use it to speculate erroneously on the true extent of Sven's patriotism vs. his loyalty.

Because let's be honest – England should beat Sweden. Look at the Football Freaking Factors ...

	FIFA rank	Population	Per capita GDP	3F
England	9	50,598,940	24,700	0.27
Sweden	14	9,001,774	23,700	1.42

And yet and yet ... It's Habitat vs. Ikea, Bentley vs. Volvo, Girls Aloud vs. Abba: one result on paper; one in reality. England have played Sweden 20 times since 1923 ... And they haven't beaten them since the ninth meeting, a friendly, back in May 1968. The one and only time they've met before in the World Cup finals was in Japan in 2002, when they drew 1:1.

Answer: ii) c
Of 1,550 official referees in Sweden, 750 are women.

How can this be explained? Perhaps these are some clues ...

Sweden has a population of about 9 million and England of about 50 million. The Swedish national stadium Råsunda has a capacity of 37,285. If Sweden had a population of 50 million and they rebuilt Råsunda scaled up to match, it would need a capacity of about 207,000. The new Wembley is set to hold 90,000.

(In September 1965, Råsunda played host to Sweden's 2:1 defeat by West Germany in what was Franz Beckenbauer's debut international game. With a crowd estimated at 52,943, the concept of health and safety was apparently unknown in Sweden at that time.)

The point is, maybe the Swedes care more about their football than the English. The question is, do the other numbers support this?

According to the Swedish FA, there are 3,275 football clubs in Sweden with a combined total of more than a million members.

---

i. If Sweden's population suddenly grew to 50 million, how many football clubs should it have pro-rata?

a) 18,194
b) 16,842
c) 19,112

And 5.55 million members nationwide ...

But, the English FA says there are 37,500 football clubs in the UK with 7 million participants.

According to the Swedish FA, there are 7,900 football pitches in Sweden.

Answer: i) a

Sweden's biggest ever victory was a 12:0 win over Latvia in 1927.

ii. If Sweden's population suddenly grew to 50 million, how many football pitches should it have pro-rata?

a) 43,888
b) 38,603
c) 31,200

The English FA says there are 45,000 football pitches in the UK.

So maybe the Swedes don't care more about football than the English after all. This time round, England are on a roll and Sven has (let's be honest) proved his commitment in spades. So thank you for the music – here at *Football Freaking* we think that this time England will claw a 1:0 win.

And why the optimism? Because Sweden's worst-ever thrashing was by England Amateur who beat them 12:1 in London on 20 October 1908, and – we're Football Freaking – so we'll pretend it's the centenary.

Close But No Cigar

In the 1930 World Cup there was no play-off for 3rd place; had there been, semi-final losers USA and Yugoslavia would have fought it out, and Yugoslavia probably would've won.

Ditto in 1950: the 3rd-place winner was decided in a league competition – but it's likely that Sweden would've beaten Spain in a play-off between semi-final losers.

The World Cup has seen 15 play-offs for 3rd place. These are the final scores. (In 1986, France beat Belgium 4:2 after extra time; the score at full-time was 2:2.)

1934	Germany vs. Austria	3:2	1978	Brazil vs. Italy	2:1
1938	Brazil vs. Sweden	4:2	1982	Poland vs. France	3:2
1954	Austria vs. Uruguay	3:1	1986	France vs. Belgium	4:2
1958	France vs. West Germany	6:3	1990	Italy vs. England	2:1
1962	Chile vs. Yugoslavia	1:0	1994	Sweden vs. Bulgaria	4:0
1966	Portugal vs. Soviet Union	2:1	1998	Croatia vs. Netherlands	2:1
1970	West Germany vs. Uruguay	1:0	2002	Turkey vs. South Korea	3:2
1974	Poland vs. Brazil	1:0			

i. On average, what was the approximate winning score in the World Cup third-place play-off?

a) 2:1
b) 3:2
c) 3:1

Who *Is* The Daddy?

Michael Owen debuted for England on Wednesday, 11 February 1998 at the age of 18 years 59 days. He scored his first goal for England later that year on 27 May in a 1:0 win over Morocco in Casablanca. At the time of writing, his 2 most recent goals for England – his 34th and his 35th, came in England's 3:2 defeat of Argentina on 12 November 2005 in Geneva.

Answer: i) a

Over a million people reputedly took to the Champs-Elysées to celebrate France's victory at the 1998 World Cup.

At the moment, Sir Bobby Charlton holds the record tally of 49 goals for England.

Assume Michael Owen continues to score goals for England at the same frequency as at 12 November 2005 ...

i. On what date would Michael Owen score his 50th goal?

a) 22 June 2012
b) 9 March 2009
c) 20 September 2015

ii. How old would Michael be on that day?

a) 35 years 319 days
b) 29 years 85 days
c) 33 years 137 days

- *Age of Sir Bobby Charlton on his last game for England: 32 years 246 days*

Michael may be the daddy and he may even be the Bobby ...

Why Not Make a Weekend of It?

The Italian Serie A contains 20 teams. As in the UK, each team plays 19 league games at home and 19 away every season.

Now imagine you've just got yourself a beautiful Italian girlfriend (or boyfriend; each to their own). You met her while she was learning English in London, but now her course has finished and she's gone home to Rome. In an

Sir Bobby Charlton scored 245 goals during the 751 games he played for Manchester United.

effort to see some football and maintain your relationship you decide to become a Roma fan for a season.

At the time of writing, EasyJet will sell you a day-return ticket for 1 adult flying from London Gatwick to Rome Ciampino airport – departing from London on a Saturday morning at 6.40 am, returning at 8.20 pm on the same evening – for £79.98 including taxes. A cheap ticket to see Roma play a Serie A home game is just £15.

i. How much would it cost to fly day-return from London to watch 19 Roma home games?

a) £2,790.44
b) £1,804.62
c) £1,388.17

- *Price of an Arsenal season ticket at the time of writing: £1,825*

(By the way, your plan failed: your Roman girlfriend dumped you after 3 matches for coming to Rome to see the football rather than her.)

Roman Will Be Nearly 60

In the first 670 days Roman Abramovich owned Chelsea, it's estimated that he spent £683.3 million on the team.

i. How much was this a day?

a) £2,567,120
b) £1,882,929
c) £1,019,851

Answers: i) b i) c

At the time of writing, Arsenal are ranked 13th in Europe and AS Roma are ranked 23rd.

At the time of writing Roman Abramovich is estimated to be worth £7.5 billion ... So now foolishly assume he'll never make another penny in capital or interest.

> **ii. For how much longer can Roman Abramovich continue to spend £1,019,851 a day on Chelsea?**
>
> a) 4,993 days
> b) 7,354 days
> c) 11,232 days

In other words, for over another 20 years – until Roman is nearly 60 years old ....

Allegedly, Roman regards Chelsea as his 'hobby' – a hobby financed through his legitimate business dealings with the Russian government, whose own assets were its legal bequest from the former USSR. Arguably, therefore, it was Communism that paid for Chelsea ... Is this where Lenin dreamt it would all end? Is this why Trotsky died on the end of an icepick in Mexico? Yep, sure looks that way ...

28.8 Billion ...

... people tuned in to watch the 2002 World Cup (as a cumulative total).

The television rights for the 2006 World Cup have been sold for £667.7 million.

Notwithstanding the appeal of games in the qualifying rounds, we'll assume this fortune is principally a payment for the rights to televise the 64 games in the finals.

Answer: ii) b

Legendary Russian goalkeeper Lev Yashin managed 480 clean sheets (59.1%) during an 812-game career.

> **i. On average, how much is ultimately being paid for each of these 64 games?**
>
> a) £32,116,000
> b) £18,994,050
> c) £10,432,812

The cumulative number of viewers for the 64 games in 2002 was 28.8 billion.

> **ii. On average, how many people viewed each game?**
>
> a) 380 million
> b) 450 million
> c) 630 million

(So if viewer numbers are the same in 2006 as they were in 2002, the price for the rights will average out to be about 2.3 pence per viewer.)

The 2002 World Cup generated 41,100 hours of dedicated TV programming worldwide.

* *4 years (the theoretical gap between each World Cup) equals: 35,064 hours*

Of National Interest

Just a week before Britain's last general election in 2005, the leaders of the country's 3 main political parties faced each other down in a televised debate hosted by Britain's premier political programme on BBC1. Essential television you might say. Duly unimpressed, a maximum of just 4.4 million of the great British public bothered tuning in.

Answers: i) c ii) b

In June 1938, the BBC broadcast the first live television pictures of a football game.

Well, perhaps most of the Great British public were off doing other things that evening? Er, nope – they just weren't interested. At the same time on a different channel, 5.8 million people were watching *Footballers' Wives*.

In that same week, the following senior league games were played in England.

Echelon	Total games	Combined crowd
Premiership	12	455,329
Championship	13	245,461
League One	13	117,419
League Two	12	69,962
Total	50	888,171

i. How many people watched *Footballers' Wives* for every two that went to a senior league football match?

a) 23
b) 18
c) 13

Frankly, that's embarrassing.

Puppy Dog Tails

In May 1960, the Chilean coast was struck by an earthquake with a magnitude of 8.5 on the Richter scale. Reputedly the largest tremor of the 20th century, it killed 5,700 people and destroyed 2 million homes. Across the Pacific Ocean, 142 Japanese were killed by the resultant tsunami.

Answer: i) c

There were 27,148,510 votes cast in the 2005 UK general election.

What an achievement it was, therefore, that just 2 years later the 1962 World Cup opened in Chile with the home team's 3:1 victory over Switzerland at the Estadio Nacional in Santiago. To quote the president of the Chilean Football Federation, Carlos Dittborn (who died a month before the first kick-off): 'We must have the World Cup because we have nothing. Since we have nothing, we will do everything.'

What is perhaps rather less of an achievement is that, against such an inspirational backdrop, the Chile World Cup also saw one of world football's most infamous and shameful moments – the notorious Battle of Santiago.

The clash, between Chile and Italy, was officiated over by legendary Essex referee Ken Aston, called in at the eleventh hour and a man who, early in his career, during the Second World War, had once abandoned a match due to a Junkers 88 bomber (rather than a dog) on (or rather over) the pitch, and who later, as chairman of the FIFA Referees Committee, would dream up the yellow and red card system (first introduced at the 1970 World Cup in Mexico) while stuck in traffic on London's Kensington High Street.

Introducing highlights of the game on BBC TV, the even-more-legendary David Coleman said: 'Good evening. The game you are about to see is the most stupid, appalling, disgusting and disgraceful exhibition of football possibly in the history of the game.'

I ask you, who could turn off after that?

Trouble had flared after Chilean newspapers accused Italian newspapers of insulting Chilean women: questioning their appeal and calling their morals into question. A conciliatory gift of carnations to the Chilean team from the Italian players immediately before the game was refused, and the die was cast ...

The first booking came after 12 seconds and the first expulsion 12 minutes in, when Italian Giorgio Ferrini was sent off for a deliberate foul. Not long after, after left-hooking the Italian captain Huberto Maschio and breaking his nose, Chile's left-back Leonel Sanchez was expelled too. When Mario David tried to drop-kick Sanchez as he left the pitch, he went with him. Three times during the 90-minute game (Aston allowed no stoppages), Ken called armed police onto the pitch. The Chileans won 2:0. What a game!

These are the number of cautions (now called yellow cards) and expulsions (now red cards) issued at each World Cup.

Competition		Cautions	Expulsions	Competition		Cautions	Expulsions
1930	Uruguay	0	1	1974	West Germany	83	4
1934	Italy	0	1	1978	Argentina	59	3
1938	France	0	3	1982	Spain	90	5
1950	Brazil	0	0	1986	Mexico	33	8
1954	Switzerland	0	3	1990	Italy	161	16
1958	Sweden	0	3	1994	USA	228	14
1962	Chile	0	6	1998	France	249	21
1966	England	20	5	2002	Korea/Japan	265	17
1970	Mexico	133	0				

After the events in Chile, referees toughened up: cautioning players far more frequently. In the 24 years between the World Cups in Chile in 1962 and Mexico in 1986 (at the 5 tournaments in England, Mexico (the first time), West Germany, Argentina and Spain), a total of 285 cautions were issued.

> **i. How many players were sent off (expelled) during this period (which included 192 World Cup games)?**
>
> a) 14
> b) 17
> c) 25

In other words, the same number of players that were sent off at the 2002 World Cup in Korea and Japan over just 64 games. Indeed, during a single

---

Answer: i) b

Referees were first allowed to use whistles in 1878.

game at Korea/Japan 2002, during the meeting between Germany and Cameroon, Spanish referee Antonio Lopez Nieto showed his yellow card to 14 players and his red to 2 players. How times change.

- *It reportedly takes 160 milliseconds (time to sprint 5 feet) for a referee to decide if a player is offside.*

A Bit Like Sven Punching Franz Beckenbauer

The Battle of Santiago wasn't the first time the World Cup ever featured a major punch-up. When Brazil lost 4:2 to Hungary in Switzerland in 1954, the game saw 2 Brazilians and a Hungarian sent off in the space of 8 minutes during the last quarter – the only expulsions of the tournament. Tempers reignited in the dressing rooms and, in a brawl involving several players, the Brazilians attacked the Hungarian staff. In reality, probably akin to current German coach Jürgen Klinsmann decking Richard Caborn MP, currently the UK Minister for Sport, the Brazilian coach Moreira thumped the Hungarian sports minister.

Competition		Number of matches	Number of cautions
1966	England	32	20
1970	Mexico	32	33
1974	West Germany	38	83
1978	Argentina	38	59
1982	Spain	52	90
1986	Mexico	52	133
1990	Italy	52	161
1994	USA	52	228
1998	France	64	249
2002	Korea/Japan	64	265

i. Including 1966, how many cautions (now yellow cards) have there been on average at each World Cup match in the last 40 years?

a) 1.35
b) 1.84
c) 2.78

Naughty, naughty? Things could have been worse. When the Marcelle coach questioned a referee's decision to caution one of his players, during a local match in Kenton-on-Sea in the Eastern Cape Province in South Africa in July 2004, the referee shot him dead, and wounded 2 of his squad.

Switzerland 1954 is cited by some as the World Cup where the game first 'got physical' – Hungary eventually lost 3:2 to West Germany in the final. In Brazil, this tournament is apparently now known as 'the Cup that Hungary lost'.

Dirty Work

The fastest-ever red card in English domestic football was earned at the start of the 2000/01 season by Sheffield Wednesday goalkeeper Kevin Pressman. He got himself sent off after just 13 seconds during his team's opening match against Wolverhampton Wanderers.

However, the dubious honour of the fastest red card in a league game anywhere, ever, is held by Joaquin Valerio, a goalie at Real Betis in the Spanish second division. Waiting in the tunnel 40 minutes before the start of a game against Albacete in December 2000, Valerios allegedly called the referee a moron, and received a red card for his trouble.

Answer: i) c
On average, 4.16 yellow cards and 0.27 red cards were issued each game at the 2002 World Cup.

The honour of successfully standing guard for the longest time in British professional football meanwhile – in other words, a goalkeeper's longest run without letting in a goal – belongs to former Rangers goalkeeper Chris Woods, who set a UK record of 1,196 minutes in 1986/87.

> ### i. At 90 minutes a game, how many games does this correspond to?
>
> a) 9.45
> b) 15.56
> c) 13.29

In the current season – 2005/06 – this would be the same as a goalie protecting his goal successfully from the start of the season in August until the start of October.

At the time of writing, the record for successfully protecting his net for the longest period overall by a league goalie anywhere belongs to Atletico de Madrid's Abel Resno who survived 1,275 minutes, until he was eventually beaten by Martinez Luis Enrique of Sporting Gijón on 19 March 1991.

> ### ii. At 90 minutes a game, how many games does this correspond to?
>
> a) 12.23
> b) 14.17
> c) 16.23

In the current season – 2005/06 – this would be the same as a goalie protecting his goal successfully from the start of the season until the middle of October.

Answers: i) c ii) b

Liverpool's Xabi Alonso's goal from 65 yards against Luton in 2006 is the longest recorded in FA Cup history.

G&T in T&T

When Trinidad and Tobago qualified for the 2006 World Cup there was, reportedly, much excitement at the British Foreign Office, which volunteered to provide consular services on behalf of the Caribbean nation in Germany. British officials were, presumably, looking forward to the briefing meetings this would necessarily entail with their counterparts in Port-of-Spain.

How crestfallen then they must have felt when it was announced that England would meet the Soca Warriors in Nuremberg on 15 June in the groups stage.

	FIFA rank	Population	Per capita GDP	3F
England	9	50,598,940	24,700	0.27
Trinidad and Tobago	51	1,088,644	9,235	10.10

It won't surprise you to learn that – however determined the crew from Port-of-Spain may be – the Football Freaking Forecast for this game is a 2:0 win to England.

Characterising the comparative enormity of the task ahead for the Trinidad and Tobago team isn't easy. But we have to try because we're Football Freaking ...

Trinidad and Tobago face 3 fixtures in the groups stage: in Dortmund, Kaiserslautern and Nuremberg.

City	Population (millions)	Stadium	Number of seats
Dortmund	0.59	FIFA World Cup Stadium	67,000
Kaiserslautern	0.10	Fritz-Walter-Stadion	48,500
Nuremberg	0.50	Franken-Stadion	45,500

i. What is the combined population of Dortmund, Kaiserslautern and Nuremberg?

a) 1,190,000
b) 1,090,000
c) 1,240,000

Put another way, the combined population of these 3 cities is greater than the entire population of Trinidad and Tobago. The combined seating of 161,000 at the 3 stadiums represents the equivalent of almost 15% of Trinidad and Tobago's population. For England, this would be, pro rata, like playing each of their matches in front of a crowd of 3 million.

Alongside the small matter of beating England and Sweden before anything else, this then is the scale of Trinidad and Tobago's task ...

Meanwhile, the Trinidad and Tobago Football Federation (TTFF) has asked its government for about £5 million to ready its team for what is the country's first World Cup. Way to go fellas: that's equivalent to £4.59 from everyone in the country including children. If the England team asked everyone in England for £4.59, they'd end up with a war chest of over £230 million. If Germany asked every one of its citizens for £4.59, they'd raise over €560 million (£379 million). Bill Clinton once said the war in Afghanistan cost America $1 billion dollars a month. If the USA asked its entire population for £4.59 it would pocket enough money to fund its Afghan campaign for nearly 2½ months.

This then is the scale of Trinidad and Tobago's commitment to the World Cup: it's war ...

Good luck Dwight.

Answer: i) a

Northern Ireland were ranked 117th in the world by FIFA when they beat England fair and square in 2005.

Paper Money ...

After the draw for the 2006 World Cup groups was held in Leipzig in December 2005, an enterprising set designer collected up the 32 pieces of paper used in the ceremony, each marked with the name of a different qualifier, and offered them for sale on eBay. Though FIFA have disputed his right to sell them, the first one – a scrap marked 'Germany' – sold for €11,250 (£7,600).

While it's unlikely the rest will sell for anything like this price, assume for a moment that they will.

---

i. How much will these 32 pieces of paper be collectively worth?

a) £456,800
b) £243,200
c) £128,400

- *At the time of writing, the best offer so far for the slip saying England is £1,750 ...*
- *A German win in the 2006 World Cup Final would earn each player a £220,000 bonus, just a place in the Final will earn them £110,000 and a knock-out from the quarter-finals £37,000*

Ouch

A warning to parents everywhere, but particularly to dads with sons: about half the hand and wrist fractures doctors see in young goalkeepers are from shots by grown-ups using an adult ball.

Answer: i) b
The first pools coupons were made by John Jervis Barnard in 1922 and developed by John Moores in 1923.

Concussion from a header is, however, an urban myth. A ball of regulation weight (14–16 ounces) would need to be travelling at over 100 mph to cause this degree of head injury (apparently). Physicists assume the ball to have an average speed of about 70 mph. A short stocky bloke can kick the ball harder than a tall one.

Assume the ball does indeed keep moving throughout a game at 70 mph (therefore 105 miles in 90 minutes) and remember a mile is 1,760 yards.

i. How many times could the ball travel up and down a 110-yard pitch in 90 minutes?

a) 780
b) 1,680
c) 1,380

And pity the assistant referees who have to run up and down the pitch alongside it ...

The Old Firm ...

... or 'Auld Firm' of Celtic and Rangers utterly dominate Scottish football. The challenge of the 'New Firm' of Aberdeen and Dundee United in the 1980s (when then plain old Alex Ferguson managed Aberdeen) is now a distant memory. Indeed, at the time of writing, the last time either team was missing from the top two of the Scottish Premier League was at the end of the season 1994/95.

Answer: i) b

The circumference of the ball was first fixed at 27–28 inches in 1872.

The two teams in the Old Firm are said to generate £120 million a year for the Scottish economy.

The Scottish population is currently about 5.1 million people.

> **i. How much does the Old Firm generate per head of the Scottish population every year?**
>
> a) £17.47
> b) £20.50
> c) £23.53

At the end of 2004, it was estimated that while English Premiership clubs had a combined operating profit of £124 million, Scottish Premier League clubs had a combined operating loss of £60 million. Coincidentally, £60 million is reputed to be Celtic's annual turnover (Rangers' is reputed to be £49 million).

Human Interest

We all love a football human interest story. Occasionally. Who could fail to have enjoyed Burton Albion's goalless draw at home against Manchester United in the FA Cup third round in 2005/06? That Burton's captain, Darren Stride, laid the paving at Burton's new Pirelli Stadium himself should be an object lesson for John Terry, Steven Gerrard and David Beckham alike.

At the forefront of Burton's thinking, as well as the game (presumably), was the estimated £800,000 some pundits suggested the club might make from the match and the Old Trafford replay (which they lost 5:0). Wayne Rooney reputedly earns £800,000 in about half a season.

Answer: i) c

24 players have 50 or more Scottish caps – on average, 61 each. Kenny Dalglish tops the list with 102 caps.

Here is a list of the players reputed to be the richest at Chelsea, Manchester United and Arsenal, and their reputed personal fortunes.

Player	Team	Fortunes (million £)
Dennis Bergkamp	Arsenal	37
Sol Campbell	Arsenal	26
Rio Ferdinand	Manchester United	20
Ryan Giggs	Manchester United	20
Ruud van Nistelrooy	Manchester United	20
Thierry Henry	Arsenal	18
Didier Drogba	Chelsea	10
Frank Lampard	Chelsea	10
Fredrik Lungberg	Arsenal	10
John Terry	Chelsea	10
Wayne Rooney	Manchester United	8

i. Based on this list, which team has the richest players on average?

a) Chelsea
b) Manchester United
c) Arsenal

ii. What is the combined fortune of the Manchester United players on this list?

a) £87 million
b) £68 million
c) £44 million

- *Estimated size of David Beckham's personal fortune: £75 million*

Answers: i) c ii) b

The male player with most international caps is the Saudi Arabian goalie Mohamed Al-Daeyea with 173.

zzzzzzzzzzzz

There are few things more galling than spending £45 on a goalless draw. Plus fares. Plus drinks and kebabs. Plus knowing the players earned a fortune for that piece of crap.

This is a list of Premiership appearances and resultant goalless draws for 20 top teams. But which team is most likely to bore you into a stupor?

Team	Premiership appearances	Goalless draws	Team	Premiership appearances	Goalless draws
Aston Villa	520	54	Coventry	354	18
Everton	519	53	Newcastle	478	17
Arsenal	519	51	Manchester United	519	16
Leeds	468	48	Charlton	241	16
Chelsea	520	47	Leicester	308	16
Blackburn	444	47	Derby	228	16
Tottenham	520	44	Sheffield Wednesday	316	16
Liverpool	518	43	Manchester City	330	15
Southampton	506	43	Fulham	166	15
Middlesbrough	398	37	Bolton	241	15

These results represent a total of 8,113 Premiership games.

i. How many goalless draws were there among these games?

a) 627
b) 815
c) 388

Answer: i) a

Blackburn have been notching up goalless draws since 1875.

So about 1 game in 13 on average. Which means any team with more goalless draws than Coventry in this list is worse than (that's more boring than) average. And on the basis of these numbers, who's most likely to condemn you to 0:0 numbness? Whisper it in Lancashire: Blackburn ...

(Whether they used to play Old Etonians or not.)

Match Abandoned Due to Atlantic on the Pitch

Here's a summary of every official 'beach soccer' World Cup match there's been so far. Where would you rather play? On a rain-soaked mud bath in the West Midlands, or on a beach in Rio?

Year	Games	Goals	Year	Games	Goals
2005	20	164	1999	20	186
2004	20	155	1998	24	219
2003	16	150	1997	16	144
2002	16	145	1996	16	131
2001	20	144	1995	16	149
2000	20	172			

i. On average how many goals have been scored in each game?

a) 8.6
b) 7.4
c) 10.2

Answer: i) a

Eric Cantona has 10 credits as a movie actor.

The average number of goals a match in any of these competitions has never been lower than 7.2.

The truth is, why should we ever put up with a goalless draw? Why can't there be this many goals in all soccer games? Discuss. (And 'Cantona' won't be accepted as your full answer.)

But Could He Lay the Paving in the Players' Tunnel?

A while back, all the chickens in the football punditry henhouse began clucking about Manchester United's loss of Vodafone as their shirt sponsor. A quick glance at who sponsored who in the English Premiership – and for how much – during the preceding 2004/05 season (see the following table) reveals why the flap may have been about more than Vodafone repositioning itself in Europe ...

Final position	Club	Shirt sponsor	Annual fee (£m)	Final position	Club	Shirt sponsor	Annual fee (£m)
1	Chelsea	Emirates	6.0	11	Charlton	all:sports	1.1
2	Arsenal	O2	5.0	12	Birmingham	FlyBe	0.75
3	Man Utd	Vodafone	9.4	13	Fulham	dabs.com	2.0
4	Everton	Chang Beer	1.5	14	Newcastle	Northern Rock	4.0
5	Liverpool	Carlsberg	5.0	15	Blackburn	HSA	1.0
6	Bolton	Reebok	2.0	16	Portsmouth	Ty	0.33
7	Middlesbrough	888.com	1.5	17	West Brom	T-Mobile	1.0
8	Man City	Thomas Cook	1.0	18	Crystal Palace	Churchill	0.3
9	Tottenham	Thomson	2.5	19	Norwich	Proton/Lotus	0.35
10	Aston Villa	DWS	2.5	20	Southampton	Friends Provident	0.5

... And why the marketing team from Thai beer Chang should have got a big fat bonus.

For the record, at the time of writing in 2005/06, Chelsea now have a deal with Samsung worth £11 million a year, the Craven Cottage boys are sporting the Pipex name for about 10% of that, and Arsenal now advertises Emirates for £5.5 million.

> ### i. What was the total value of shirt sponsorship in the Premiership in 2004/05?
>
> a) £35.22 million
> b) £60.55 million
> c) £47.73 million

- *Amount Anheuser-Busch paid for beer rights to 2006 World Cup: £22.6 million*
- *Amount Jose Mourinho believes John Terry's transfer value would be: £50 million*

Invisible Prize

Amid all the talk of cup-tie and TV deals it's often easy to forget that the Premiership is worth a barrel of cash in prizes itself ...

This is a list of how much each of the Premiership teams came away with at the end of the 2002/03 season.

Final position	Club	Premiership prize money (£)	Final position	Club	Premiership prize money (£)
1	Manchester United	10,060,000	11	Middlesbrough	5,030,000
2	Arsenal	9,557,000	12	Charlton Athletic	4,527,000
3	Newcastle United	9,054,000	13	Birmingham City	4,024,000
4	Chelsea	8,551,000	14	Fulham	3,521,000
5	Liverpool	8,048,000	15	Leeds United	3,018,000
6	Blackburn Rovers	7,545,000	16	Aston Villa	2,515,000
7	Everton	7,042,000	17	Bolton Wanderers	2,012,000
8	Southampton	6,539,000	18	West Ham United	1,509,000
9	Manchester City	6,036,000	19	West Bromwich Albion	1,006,000
10	Tottenham Hotspur	5,533,000	20	Sunderland	503,000

Answer: i) c

In 2005/06, European football-shirt sponsorship totalled about £232.3 million.

i. What was the total prize money available?

a) £91,345,000
b) £105,630,000
c) £124,760,000

Divided equally between the 20 teams, this would yield £5,281,500 each. Teams winning more than that, they beat the odds, less and they didn't. As we can see from these figures, Tottenham at position 10 is pretty close to the dividing line. The striking difference is that between position 1 and position 20.

- *Amount* Harry Potter and the Goblet of Fire *made in 3 days (in 21 countries): £105 million*

- *Wage Chelsea have allegedly offered Michael Ballack: £121,000 a week*

Visible Prize

Of course the one 'prize' every big club seems to endlessly squeal about is the one you'd need to be a hermit not to know about: their share of the TV money.

This is a list of how much each of the Premiership teams came away with from that barrel of cash at the end of the 2002/03 season.

Answer: i) b
Every year in England, 75 professional players face premature retirement through injury.

Final position	Club	TV facility fee (£)*	Final position	Club	TV facility fee (£)*
1	Manchester United	11,460,000	11	Middlesbrough	4,400,000
2	Arsenal	9,890,000	12	Charlton Athletic	3,180,000
3	Newcastle United	7,100,000	13	Birmingham City	4,450,000
4	Chelsea	6,350,000	14	Fulham	3,270,000
5	Liverpool	9,690,000	15	Leeds United	4,700,000
6	Blackburn Rovers	3,970,000	16	Aston Villa	4,310,000
7	Everton	4,330,000	17	Bolton Wanderers	3,990,000
8	Southampton	2,980,000	18	West Ham United	5,200,000
9	Manchester City	3,960,000	19	West Bromwich Albion	2,980,000
10	Tottenham Hotspur	5,650,000	20	Sunderland	4,280,000

* Based on number of TV appearances (on Sky and ITV1)

i. What was the total TV fee money available?

a) £57,340,000
b) £207,220,000
c) £106,140,000

Divided equally between the 20 teams, this would yield £5,307,000 each. Teams receiving more than that beat the odds, less and they didn't. With the exception of Tottenham, only the top 5 teams managed this.

Answer: i) c

TV rights to all FIFA games between 2007 and 2014 were recently sold in the USA for just US $425 million.

We're Calling Him The Young Player of the Year, But He's Only 20 Years Old

600 16-year-olds join the English game full time each year; 500 have left it by the age of 21.

The average age of the England squad who turned out for a friendly against Argentina in the months preceding the 2006 World Cup was 26 years 6 months 28 days.

Assume this England squad all began their careers at the age of 16 ...

i. How many 16-year-olds have joined the English game full time by the time a player reaches the England squad's average age?

a) 6,000
b) 8,000
c) 4,000

ii. And at least how many will have left the game?

a) 4,000
b) 3,000
c) 2,000

All the ex-players I meet are builders or cab drivers.

George Weah, European Footballer of the Year 1995, narrowly lost the Liberian Presidential election in 2005.

Crunching Tackle

As the face of Walkers Crisps, Gary Lineker reputedly earns £1.5 million a year.

---

i. At £0.35 for a 34.5 g packet, how many packets of crisps are equivalent to Gary's fee?

a) 4,285,714
b) 2,142,857
c) 6,428,571

It takes Walkers (a subsidiary of Pepsico) about 18 hours to manufacture this many bags.

Each 35p (ready salted) pack contains 11.7 g of fat.

---

ii. How many grams of fat do £1.5 million worth of ready salted crisps contain?

a) 12,321,428
b) 24,642,856
c) 50,142,854

There are two ways to consider this result. In the first, this is equivalent to about 0.84 g of fat for every man, woman and child in the UK. In the second – if a man weighs 79.2 kg on average – Walkers must sell the British public fats equivalent in weight to about 633 average men to raise Gary's fee.

Answers: i) a ii) c

Walkers manufacture over 4,000 packets of crisps every minute.

Good fundamentals

Doing its bit for Germany during the run-up to World Cup 2006, the Nuremberg Centre for Further Education offered students a course run by former women's Bundesliga star Vittoria Coppolecchia called: 'Understanding Football – Now It's Women's Turn!'

Run for women keen to understand more about the game, the exercise aimed, reportedly, 'to empower women in the home environment with an equal voice in the endless debates about football'. So there. And it's not funny.

At the time of writing, the combined annual income of the world's five best remunerated women soccer players is reported to be just US $525,000 (£296,500) mainly from sports brand sponsorship. So, allowing for 40% more, if women could pull in the bigger crowd the men bring, that goes up to £415,000. Accept that women, in the UK at least, earn 75% of what men earn for comparable full-time work and allow for that too. The total remuneration package of the world's five best-remunerated women soccer players should therefore be worth about £553,000.

Frank Lampard reputedly earns £100,000 per week.

> **i. How many days does it take Frank Lampard to earn £553,000?**
>
> a) 55
> b) 10
> c) 39

What glaringly obvious conclusion can *Football Freaking* draw from this? Easy. Women, you work cheap!

This is the lesson *Football Freaking* would teach the class in Nuremberg if it were invited in as a guest lecturer ...

Answer: i) c

The women's world record for keepie uppie is 55,187 touches. It was set by Fiamma Monza player Milene Domingues.

Preferable to Rotherham at Home? You Decide ...

During the 32 games of the Women's World Cup in the USA in 2003, there were 107 goals scored.

i. How many goals was that on average a game?
a) 3.04
b) 3.64
c) 3.34

Historically, the average number of goals in a men's World Cup match is 2.95.

In the men's 2002 World Cup, there were 161 goals in 64 games, an average of 2.52 goals a game.

So the women's games must have been more fun to watch.

The October 2003 Women's World Cup Final went to 2:1 after extra time to Germany against Sweden. It was watched by a crowd of 90,185 fans.

At the time of writing, the average gate at Rotherham United during the 2005/06 season so far has been 4,782.

The question is, based on relative attendance, how many more times did this Women's World Cup final appear to appeal to people than does an average Rotherham United game? But this question is too long for a question box. So ...

ii. What is the answer to the question?
a) 19
b) 22
c) 15

Answers: i) c ii) a

The female player with most international caps is Kristine Lilly, the US Women's National Team captain, with a record 300.

Bastard Ref

The first team ever to represent Wales on the international stage ran out to a 4:0 defeat by Scotland in Glasgow on 25 March 1876. The Welsh team included two lawyers, a clerk, a soldier, a miner, a timber merchant, a student, a stone-mason, a medical doctor, a chimney sweep and an insurance salesman. One of Scotland's goals was scored by a shipyard worker nicknamed Reddie; a player burdened by the improbable challenge of having only one eye. It may be some consolation, if you're Welsh, to know that Reddie somehow kept his monocular vision secret when later he transferred from Clydesdale to Sheffield Wednesday.

Wales first played England 3 years later, in London, on 18 January 1879. Both teams and the referee, one Segard Richard Bastard, agreed the game should be cut to two halves of 30 minutes each because the weather was so dreadful – so dreadful the England wing-half, travelling from Sheffield, failed to make the game until a full 20 minutes after kick-off. England were obliged to start short-handed, but Wales still lost 2:1.

At the end of the 2004/05 season, the last season for which figures are available, the Vauxhall Masterfit Retailers Welsh Premier League was topped by Total Network Solutions (such lyrical names; it's easy to see why Wales has such a reputation for poetry) by 4 clear points. During the season, 892 goals were scored in 306 games.

> **i. On average, how many goals were scored in each game of the Vauxhall Masterfit Retailers Welsh Premier League?**
>
> a) 2.92
> b) 1.88
> c) 3.12

Answer: i) a

In Sweden in 1958, Wales lost 1:0 to Brazil in the World Cup quarter-finals. They haven't done so well since.

So slightly less goals on average than a men's World Cup game, but markedly less than in the Women's World Cup, and a lot less than in the beach World Cup ...

Fish in a Barrel

These are 10 of the world's most prolific scorers ever in single seasons of the senior game ...

Rank	Player	Country	Season	Matches	Goals
1	Archibald McPherson Stark	USA	1924/25	44	67
2	Ferenc Deák	Hungary	1945/46	34	66
3	William Ralph Dean	England	1927/28	39	60
4	Héctor Horace Scotta	Argentina	1975	57	60
5	Refik Resmja	Albania	1951	23	59
6	Ferenc Deák	Hungary	1948/49	30	59
7	Edson Arantes do Nascimento (Pelé)	Brazil	1958	38	58
8	José Saturnino Cardozo	Paraguay	2002/03	42	58
9	Josef Bican	*	1943/44	23	57
10	Guyla Zsengellér	Hungary	1938/39	26	56

* Protectorate of Bohemia and Moravia (now Czech Republic)

Assume there are 90 minutes in each match.

i. On average, how often in minutes did these guys score?

a) 42.5
b) 53.4
c) 74.3

Answer: i) b

The first game recorded between women in Scotland was in 1892, the first recorded in England, in 1895.

In 2004/05 the highest scorer in the English Premiership was Arsenal's Thierry Henry, with 25 goals for the season.

Carpe Diem

He who laughs last may laugh longest, but this is certainly not true for he who scores last.

Using results from 168 games, this table lists how often each team in the English Premiership scored first. Then it lists how many of these games each team went on to win, draw or lose. For example, looking at the table, Aston Villa scored first in 9 games of which, ultimately, they won 5, drew 3 and lost 1.

We'll use this list as a sample of games with which to explore the importance of an early lead.

	Total games	Wins	Draws	Losses
Chelsea	16	16	0	0
Manchester United	13	10	3	0
Liverpool	12	11	1	0
Bolton Wanderers	11	8	2	1
Tottenham Hotspur	10	7	3	0
Fulham	10	4	3	3
Arsenal	9	8	0	1
Everton	9	6	2	1
Aston Villa	9	5	3	1
Portsmouth	9	2	3	4
Wigan Athletic	8	8	0	0
Newcastle United	8	6	2	0
Blackburn Rovers	7	6	0	1
Charlton Athletic	7	6	0	1
Manchester City	6	5	0	1
Middlesbrough	5	3	2	0
Birmingham City	5	3	0	2
West Ham United	5	3	0	2
Sunderland	5	0	2	3
West Bromwich Albion	4	3	0	1

i. How many of these games did the team that scored first eventually win?

a) 135
b) 166
c) 120

Over 71% of games.

ii. How many of these games did the team that scored first eventually lose?

a) 19
b) 22
c) 28

Around 13% of games.

Scoring first is obviously vital: a team that scores first in the English Premiership appears to win nearly 6 times more frequently than it will lose.

At the 2002 World Cup meanwhile, only 60% of finals games were eventually won by the team that scored first. Based on this data therefore, national sides would appear to be better at pulling back from behind than club sides.

First Blood

James Vaughn became the youngest player ever to score in the English Premiership when he knocked one in for Everton against Crystal Palace on 10 April 2005. He was 16 years 271 days.

Answers: i) c ii) b

1997 FA Cup Final: Chelsea's Roberto di Matteo scores after 43 seconds. Wembley's fastest FA Cup Final goal ever. Chelsea win.

It's a record that has slowly been coming down over the last 9 years.

Player	Date	Fixture	Age
Michael Owen	06.05.97	Liverpool vs. Wimbledon	17 years 144 days
Wayne Rooney	19.10.02	Everton vs. Arsenal	16 years 361 days
James Milner	26.12.02	Leeds vs. Sunderland	16 years 357 days

To break this record, the next record breaker must be younger than 16 years 270 days.

Come 9 June 2006, the opening day of the World Cup, what is the earliest possible date of birth you could have to still be able to break this record?

i. In other words, what is your date of birth if you were 16 years 270 days old on 9 June 2006?

a) Wednesday, 13 September 1989
b) Tuesday, 16 June 1991
c) Friday, 3 September 1988

And if your birthday was before then? Forget it.

Football Widows

During the run-up to the 2002 World Cup, an England FA spokesman – presumably in a dual attempt to prick masculine pride and drum up desperately needed ticket sales – claimed lacklustre interest was due to 'nagging-wife syndrome', suggesting men don't go to football because their wives won't let them.

Answer: i) a

Everton was the first team ever to wear the numbers 1–11; Dixie Dean was the first-ever number 9.

The evidence though is the frau tends to lose to the footie. Take the London housewife whose man took a fortnight's holiday to watch Euro 2004 in the pub with his pals; her divorce petition claimed he'd attended every home game his team had played since his wedding day. (Yeh; and so?)

Football Freaking knows not how this tragic story ended. But if it was in the divorce courts, it can hazard a guess what the court awarded her: £13,000 is about the UK average.

So when a Middlesbrough midfielder was divorced by his wife for playing away (sorry), the landmark case saw her awarded £1.8 million – further proof, if any were needed, that footballers' wives aren't like other people.

---

i. How many average football widows' divorce settlements could be funded by this single payment to a footballer's wife?

a) 176
b) 138
c) 100

David Beckham has a personal fortune estimated at £75 million.

---

ii. At an average of £1.8 million a time, how many divorce settlements could David afford?

a) 41
b) 31
c) 51

Not that he's told us if he's planning a divorce.

Answers: i) b ii) a

On average, a high-street solicitor charges £800 plus VAT to process an uncontested divorce.

Deadeyed Dicks

These were the 8 most effective goal scorers in the world in 2005; the men who grabbed the most goals from the fewest games.

Player	Club	Country	Goals	Games
Rubén Darío Aguilera	San José Orura	Paraguay	20	18
Clémerson de Araújo Soares	Gamba Osaka	Brazil	33	33
Martin Kambourov	FC Lokomotiv Plovdiv	Bulgaria	27	29
Fatih Tekke	Trabzonspor K Trabzon	Turkey	31	34
Collins Mbesuma	Kaiser Chiefs Johannesburg	Zambia	25	28
Dirk Kuijt	Feyenoord Rotterdam	Netherlands	29	34
Guillermo Franco	CF Monterrey	Argentina	23	28
Liédson da Silva Nuniz	Sporting Clube de Portugal Lisboa	Brazil	25	31

i. Between them, how many goals did the world's best score a match on average?

a) 1.122
b) 0.906
c) 0.778

Here are comparable figures from the English Premiership.

Player	Club	Goals	Games
Thierry Henry	Arsenal	25	31
Andrew Johnson	Crystal Palace	21	37
Robert Pires	Arsenal	14	26
Jermain Defoe	Tottenham	13	28
Aiyegbeni Yakubu	Portsmouth	13	29
Andy Cole	Fulham	12	29
Jimmy Floyd Hasselbaink	Middlesbrough	13	36
Frank Lampard	Chelsea	13	38

Answer: i) b

Goal kicks were first introduced in 1869.

(Obviously Thierry Henry is also 8th equal in the world.)

ii. Between them, how many goals did the English Premiership's best score a match on average?

a) 0.394
b) 0.488
c) 0.667

This suggests the best in the world are 85.7% better than the best in the English Premiership.

Pasta Vs. Paella

As to the rest of them ...

Here are the scoring records of the top 8 goal scorers in both the Spanish Premera Liga and Italian Serie A at the end of the 2004/05 season.

As before, scores are ranked in terms of goals per game.

Spanish Premera Liga				Italian Serie A			
Player	Club	Goals	Matches	Player	Club	Goals	Matches
Diego Forlan	Villarreal	25	31	Mirko Vucinic	Lecce	19	20
Luiz Ronaldo	Real Madrid	21	32	Christiano Lucarelli	Livorno	24	33
Samuel Eto'o	Barcelona	24	37	Vincenzo Montella	Roma	22	34
Ricardo Oliveira	Real Betis	22	36	Leite Adriano	Inter Milan	16	25
Cesar Baptista	FC Sevilla	18	30	Alberto Gilardino	Parma	24	38
Juan Riquelme	Villarreal	15	31	Andriy Shevchenko	AC Milan	17	27
Rodriguez Maxi	Espanyol	15	34	Luca Toni	Palermo	20	35
Fernando Torres	Atletico Madrid	16	37	Mauro Esposito	Cagliari	16	33

Answer: ii) b

With the capacity for 100,000 spectators, Camp Nou, home of FC Barcelona, is the largest stadium in Europe.

The collective match totals are 268 games for the Spanish scorers, and 245 for the Italian.

---

i. Between them, how many goals are the Spanish Premera's best 8 scoring per match on average?

a) 0.71
b) 0.58
c) 0.44

---

ii. Between them, how many goals are the Italian Serie A's best 8 scoring per match on average?

a) 0.69
b) 0.64
c) 0.75

So to see the best footie, you're better getting an Italian girlfriend and commuting to Italy than a Spanish girlfriend and commuting to Spain. But as to anything else ...

Drinkers Vs. Smokers

And in those countries where they know what mud really means ...

Here are the scoring records of the top 8 goal scorers in both the German Bundesliga and the Dutch Eredivisie at the end of the 2004/05 season.

Answers: i) b ii) b

Italy have played Spain 7 times and won 3, drawn 3 and lost 1. Aggregate score – 8:7 to Italy.

German Bundesliga

Player	Club	Goals	Matches
Marek Mintal	Nurnberg	24	30 est.
Roy Makaay	Bayern München	33	22
Dimitar Berbatov	Bayer Leverkusen	20	32
Andrej Voronin	Bayer Leverkusen	15	25
Marcelo Marcelinho	Hertha Berlin	18	32
Jan Koller	Borussia Dortmund	15	27
Miroslav Klose	Werder Bremen	15	28
Delron Buckley	Arminia Bielefeld	15	29

Dutch Eredivisie

Player	Club	Goals	Matches
Dirk Kuijt	Feyenoord Rotterdam	29	34
Erik Nevland	FC Groningen	16	20
Salomon Kalou	Feyenoord Rotterdam	20	26
Jan Vennegoor of Hesselink	PSV Eindhoven	19	26
Klaas-Jan Huntelaar	Heerenveen	17	31
Blaise N'Kufo	Twente Enschede	16	32
Mark Van Bommel	PSV Eindhoven	14	30
Arouna Kone	Roda JC Kerkrade	14	32

The collective match totals are 236 games and 231 for the Dutch.

i. Between them, how many goals did the German top 8 score a match on average?

a) 0.33
b) 0.61
c) 0.99

Answer: i) b

It's estimated that over 240 million people regularly play football worldwide (and although they may not realise it, even more Number Freak).

ii. Between them, how many goals did the Dutch top 8 score a match on average?

a) 0.69
b) 0.63
c) 0.66

Which suggests the Eredivisie is more exciting than the Bundesliga (and may or may not confirm the old saw that smokers are more interesting people).

In their last 14 meetings (at the time of writing), the German and Dutch national teams have both won 4 times. The Dutch lead by an aggregate score of 20:19.

Ah Yes, the French ...

Here are the scoring records of the top 8 goal scorers in the French Ligue 1 at the end of the 2004/05 season after a combined total of 238 games.

Player	Club	Goals	Matches
Alexander Frei	Rennes	20	31
Mickael Pagis	Strasbourg	15	30
Matt Moussilou	Lille	12	24
Pedro Pauleta	PSG	14	30
Sebastien Mazure	Caen	13	28
Pernambucano Juninho	Lyon	13	30
Mamadou Niang	Strasbourg	12	30
Pascal Feindouno	St Etienne	13	35

Answer: ii) b

The newest member of FIFA is Comoros, which joined in 2005. Its FA was formed in 1979.

i. Between them, how many goals did the French Ligue 1's best 8 score a match on average?

a) 0.95

b) 0.47

c) 0.22

Not many when you consider the comparable result in Serie A is 37% higher at 0.64.

The following table summarises and ranks the top European leagues in order of the scoring record of their top 8 scorers during the 2004/05 season.

Rank	Top 8 league scorers from ...	Goals	Games
1	Italian Serie A	158	245
2	Dutch Eredivisie	145	231
3	German Bundesliga	144	236
4	Spanish Premera	156	268
5	Scottish Premier League	140	254
6	English Premiership	124	254
7	French Ligue 1	112	238
Total		979	1726

This then is *Football Freaking*'s ranking of the 7 major European leagues according to how exciting they are. Contrary to an earlier conclusion, it looks like English football isn't the dullest after all. Its' the, er, French ...

ii. How many goals did the best 8 of all these 7 leagues score a match on average between them?

a) 0.48

b) 0.66

c) 0.57

Answers: i) b ii) c

The world's top scorer in 2004/05 with 33 goals from 33 games was Clémerson de Araújo Soares of Brazil.

Just as a comparative reminder, the world's 8 most effective scorers scored 0.91 goals a match on average (or 60% more than the best scorers in Europe).

Football Freaking's 10 Favourite FA Cup Upsets

1951	Round 3	Worcester City vs. Liverpool	2:1
1957	Round 4	Bournemouth & Boscombe Athletic vs. Tottenham Hotspur	3:1
1972	Round 3	Hereford United vs. Newcastle United	2:1
1978	Round 3	Blyth Spartans vs. Stoke City	3:2
1986	Round 3	Birmingham City vs. Altrincham	1:2
1989	Round 3	Sutton United vs. Coventry City	2:1
1991	Round 3	Wrexham vs. Arsenal	2:1
2001	Quarter-final	Leicester City vs. Wycombe Wanderers	1:2
2003	Round 3	Shrewsbury Town vs. Everton	2:1
2006	Round 3	Manchester United vs. Burton Albion	0:0

i. In these games, what was the average score by which the plucky little underdog beat the strutting peacock?

a) 2:0
b) 1:0
c) 2:1

And why are these particular upsets our favourites? Because the one thing all Football Freakers know is that the numbers can always surprise you ...

Answer: i) c
06.01.74 FA Cup third round: Oldham win, Cambridge United lose the first ever Sunday game in England 1:0.

As this book is being finished, the 2006 World Cup in Germany is just around the corner. Never has there been a better time to be a Football Freaker. Why? Because football isn't rocket science anymore. Financial doping at Chelsea has proved it can be done: to paraphrase über management consultants McKinseys, having been measured, nowadays football can be managed.

The remainder of this book lists *Football Freaking*'s copper-bottomed forecasts for the 2006 World Cup. Why not see how we got on? Then grab the real results by the throat and see what you can Football Freak with them ...

Chances of winning the World Cup – Bookmakers odds					
Brazil	11/4	Mexico	50/1	South Korea	250/1
England	11/2	Ukraine	66/1	Tunisia	250/1
Argentina	7/1	Croatia	80/1	Ecuador	300/1
Germany	7/1	Australia	100/1	Japan	300/1
Italy	9/1	Ivory Coast	100/1	Angola	400/1
France	12/1	Poland	100/1	Togo	400/1
Holland	12/1	USA	100/1	Costa Rica	500/1
Spain	14/1	Serbia/Montenegro	125/1	Iran	500/1
Portugal	22/1	Switzerland	125/1	Saudi Arabia	1000/1
Czech Republic	28/1	Ghana	200/1	Trinidad and	
Sweden	33/1	Paraguay	250/1	Tobago	1000/1

And it doesn't have to stop here. Come Euro 2008 and the 2010 World Cup, and every other match before or after, there can still be Football Freaking.

All you have to do is make them up as you go along ...

And if you want? Feel free to post them online at www.footballfreaking.co.uk

Football Freaking Forecasts for the 2006 World Cup

Group A

	FIFA rank	Population	Per capita GDP €	Single airfare to Munich €	Football Freaking Factor (3F)
Germany	16	82,431,390	23,950	---	---
Costa Rica	21	4,016,173	8,010	1,375.9	6.53
Poland	23	38,557,984	10,015	578.4	2.19
Ecuador	37	13,363,593	3,090	1,915.5	23.56

Date	Kick-off	Match	Forecast	Venue
Fri 9 June	18:00	Germany vs. Costa Rica	2:0	Munich
Fri 9 June	21:00	Poland vs. Ecuador	2:1	Gelsenkirchen
Wed 14 June	21:00	Germany vs. Poland	1:0	Dortmund
Thu 15 June	15:00	Ecuador vs. Costa Rica	3:3	Hamburg
Tue 20 June	16:00	Ecuador vs. Germany	1:4	Berlin
Tue 20 June	16:00	Costa Rica vs. Poland	2:2	Hanover

Team	MP	W	D	L	GF	GA	Pts	
Germany	3	3	0	0	7	1	9	W
Costa Rica	3	0	2	1	5	7	2	
Poland	3	1	1	1	4	4	4	R
Ecuador	3	0	1	2	5	9	1	

Group A winner: Germany
Group A runner-up: Poland

Over 400,000 Poles play football regularly.

Football Freaking Forecasts for the 2006 World Cup – *continued*

| Group B | | | | |

	FIFA rank	Population	Per capita GDP €	Single airfare to Munich €	Football Freaking Factor (3F)
England	9	50,598,940	24,700	176.5	0.27
Paraguay	30	6,347,884	4,005	701.9	6.66
Trinidad and Tobago	51	1,088,644	9,235	2,454.2	10.10
Sweden	14	9,001,774	23,700	884.3	1.42

Date	Kick-off	Match	Forecast	Venue
Sat 10 June	15:00	England vs. Paraguay	1:1	Frankfurt
Sat 10 June	18:00	Trinidad and Tobago vs. Sweden	0:1	Dortmund
Thu 15 June	18:00	England vs. Trinidad and Tobago	2:0	Nuremberg
Thu 15 June	21:00	Sweden vs. Paraguay	1:1	Berlin
Tue 20 June	21:00	Paraguay vs. Trinidad and Tobago	3:0	Kaiserslautern
Tue 20 June	21:00	Sweden vs. England	0:1	Cologne

Team	MP	W	D	L	GF	GA	Pts	
England	3	2	1	0	4	1	7	W
Paraguay	3	1	2	0	5	2	5	R
Trinidad and Tobago	3	0	0	3	0	6	0	
Sweden	3	1	1	1	2	2	4	

Group B winner: England
Group B runner-up: Paraguay

Paraguay also reached the second round in 1998 and 2002.

Football Freaking Forecasts for the 2006 World Cup - *continued*

Group C

	FIFA rank	Population	Per capita GDP €	Single airfare to Munich €	Football Freaking Factor (3F)
Argentina	4	39,537,943	10,350	822.3	3.02
Côte d'Ivoire	41	17,298,040	1,250	1,774.7	53.95
Serbia and Montenegro	47	10,829,175	2,000	733.2	13.93
Netherlands	3	16,407,491	9,515	730.1	2.92

Date	Kick-off	Match	Forecast	Venue
Sat 10 June	21:00	Argentina vs. Côte d'Ivoire	4:0	Hamburg
Sun 11 June	15:00	Serbia and Montenegro vs. Netherlands	1:1	Leipzig
Fri 16 June	15:00	Argentina vs. Serbia and Montenegro	3:1	Gelsenkirchen
Fri 16 June	18:00	Netherlands vs. Côte d'Ivoire	2:0	Stuttgart
Wed 21 June	21:00	Netherlands vs. Argentina	2:3	Frankfurt
Wed 21 June	21:00	Côte d'Ivoire vs. Serbia and Montenegro	2:1	Munich

Team	MP	W	D	L	GF	GA	Pts	
Argentina	3	3	0	0	10	3	9	W
Côte d'Ivoire	3	1	0	2	2	7	3	
Serbia and Montenegro	3	0	1	2	3	6	1	
Netherlands	3	1	1	1	5	4	4	R

Group C winner: Argentina
Group C runner-up: Netherlands

> The first-ever Dutch football club, Haarlemsche Football Club (HFC), was founded in 1879.

Football Freaking Forecasts for the 2006 World Cup – *continued*

Group D					
	FIFA rank	Population	Per capita GDP €	Single airfare to Munich €	Football Freaking Factor (3F)
Mexico	7	106,202,903	8,010	1,515.9	7.19
Iran	19	68,017,860	6,425	394.5	2.33
Angola	62	11,827,315	1,750	1,769.0	38.41
Portugal	10	10,566,212	14,940	391.1	0.99

Date	Kick-off	Match	Forecast	Venue
Sun 11 June	18:00	Mexico vs. Iran	2:2	Nuremberg
Sun 11 June	21:00	Angola vs. Portugal	1:2	Cologne
Fri 16 June	21:00	Mexico vs. Angola	2:1	Hanover
Sat 17 June	15:00	Portugal vs. Iran	2:2	Frankfurt
Wed 21 June	16:00	Portugal vs. Mexico	2:1	Gelsenkirchen
Wed 21 June	16:00	Iran vs. Angola	3:1	Leipzig

Team	MP	W	D	L	GF	GA	Pts	
Mexico	3	1	1	1	5	5	4	
Iran	3	1	2	0	7	5	5	R
Angola	3	0	0	3	6	4	0	
Portugal	3	2	1	0	6	4	7	W

Group D winner: Portugal
Group D runner-up: Iran

Angola gained its independence from Portugal on Remembrance Day, Tuesday, 11 November 1975.

Football Freaking Forecasts for the 2006 World Cup – *continued*

Group E

	FIFA rank	Population	Per capita GDP €	Single airfare to Munich €	Football Freaking Factor (3F)
Italy	12	58,103,033	23,120	713.1	1.17
Ghana	50	21,946,247	1,900	1,927.4	38.55
United States	8	295,734,134	33,450	2,015.3	2.29
Czech Republic	2	10,241,138	14,780	584.4	1.50

Date	Kick-off	Match	Forecast	Venue
Mon 12 June	21:00	Italy vs. Ghana	1:1	Hanover
Mon 12 June	18:00	USA vs. Czech Republic	0:1	Gelsenkirchen
Sat 17 June	21:00	Italy vs. USA	0:0	Kaiserslautern
Sat 17 June	18:00	Czech Republic vs. Ghana	4:2	Cologne
Thu 22 June	16:00	Czech Republic vs. Italy	2:2	Hamburg
Thu 22 June	16:00	Ghana vs. USA	2:1	Nuremberg

Team	MP	W	D	L	GF	GA	Pts	
Italy	3	0	3	0	3	2	3	
Ghana	3	1	1	1	5	6	4	R
USA	3	0	1	2	2	2	1	
Czech Republic	3	2	1	0	6	4	7	W

Group E winner: Czech Republic
Group E runner-up: Ghana

Ghanaian Michael Essien is Africa's most expensive footballer, reportedly bought by Chelsea for £26 million.

Football Freaking Forecasts for the 2006 World Cup – *continued*

Group F

	FIFA rank	Population	Per capita GDP €	Single airfare to Munich €	Football Freaking Factor (3F)
Brazil	1	186,112,794	6,760	1,286.8	7.23
Croatia	20	4,495,904	9,350	974.7	3.96
Australia	49	20,090,437	27,000	809.5	1.14
Japan	15	127,417,244	24,500	2,913.1	4.52

Date	Kick-off	Match	Forecast	Venue
Mon 12 June	15:00	Australia vs. Japan	2:1	Kaiserslautern
Tues 13 June	21:00	Brazil vs. Croatia	3:0	Berlin
Sun 18 June	18:00	Brazil vs. Australia	2:0	Munich
Sun 18 June	15:00	Japan vs. Croatia	1:0	Nuremberg
Thu 22 June	21:00	Japan vs. Brazil	1:3	Dortmund
Thu 22 June	21:00	Croatia vs. Australia	0:1	Stuttgart

Team	MP	W	D	L	GF	GA	Pts	
Brazil	3	3	0	0	8	1	9	W
Croatia	3	0	0	3	0	5	0	
Australia	3	2	0	1	3	3	6	R
Japan	3	1	0	2	3	5	3	

Group F winner: Brazil
Group F runner-up: Australia

> **At the 1974 World Cup in Germany, Australia lost twice to the Germans –
> 3:0 to the West and 2:0 to the East.**

Football Freaking Forecasts for the 2006 World Cup – *continued*

Group G

	FIFA rank	Population	Per capita GDP €	Single airfare to Munich €	Football Freaking Factor (3F)
France	5	60,656,178	23,950	574.0	0.91
Switzerland	36	7,489,370	29,730	334.5	0.48
South Korea	29	48,640,671	16,025	3,719.0	8.82
Togo	56	5,399,991	1,335	1,795.9	51.12

Date	Kick-off	Match	Forecast	Venue
Tue 13 June	18:00	France vs. Switzerland	1:0	Stuttgart
Tue 13 June	15:00	South Korea vs. Togo	3:0	Frankfurt
Sun 18 June	21:00	France vs. South Korea	2:0	Leipzig
Mon 19 June	15:00	Togo vs. Switzerland	2:1	Dortmund
Fri 23 June	21:00	Switzerland vs. South Korea	2:2	Hanover
Fri 23 June	21:00	Togo vs. France	0:4	Cologne

Team	MP	W	D	L	GF	GA	Pts	
France	3	3	0	0	7	0	9	W
Switzerland	3	0	1	2	3	5	1	
South Korea	3	1	1	1	5	4	4	R
Togo	3	1	0	2	2	8	3	

Group G winner: France
Group G runner-up: South Korea

The Taeguk Warriors biggest-ever international win? In 2003, South Korea beat Nepal 16:0 at home.

Football Freaking Forecasts for the 2006 World Cup – *continued*

| Group H | | | | |

	FIFA rank	Population	Per capita GDP €	Single airfare to Munich €	Football Freaking Factor (3F)
Spain	6	40,341,462	20,490	121.3	0.22
Ukraine	40	46,996,765	5,250	878.5	6.36
Tunisia	28	10,074,951	5,925	325.5	2.09
Saudi Arabia	32	26,417,599	10,015	1,373.7	5.21

Date	Kick-off	Match	Forecast	Venue
Wed 14 June	15:00	Spain vs. Ukraine	1:2	Leipzig
Wed 14 June	18:00	Tunisia vs. Saudi Arabia	2:0	Munich
Mon 19 June	21:00	Spain vs. Tunisia	0:0	Stuttgart
Mon 19 June	18:00	Saudi Arabia vs. Ukraine	2:2	Hamburg
Fri 23 June	16:00	Ukraine vs. Tunisia	0:2	Berlin
Fri 23 June	16:00	Saudi Arabia vs. Spain	0:2	Kaiserslautern

Team	MP	W	D	L	GF	GA	Pts	
Spain	3	1	1	1	3	2	4	R
Ukraine	3	1	1	1	4	5	4	
Tunisia	3	2	1	0	4	0	7	W
Saudi Arabia	3	0	1	2	2	6	1	

Group H winner: Tunisia
Group H runner-up: Spain

The shortest-ever World Cup career was Tunisia's Khemais Labidi's 2 minutes against Mexico in 1978.

Football Freaking Forecasts for the 2006 World Cup - *continued*

Second Round

	Date	Kick-off	Match	Forecast	Venue
1.	Sat 24 June	17:00	Germany vs. Paraguay	4:3 pso	Munich

Previous games

15.06.02	Germany vs. Paraguay	1:0 (0:0)	2002 World Cup

	Date	Kick-off	Match	Forecast	Venue
2.	Sat 24 June	21:00	Argentina vs. Iran	4:0	Leipzig

Previous games – None

	Date	Kick-off	Match	Forecast	Venue
3.	Sun 25 June	17:00	England vs. Poland	2:1	Stuttgart

Previous games

12.10.05	England vs. Poland	2:1 (1:1)	2006 World Cup Prelim
08.09.04	Poland vs. England	1:2 (0:1)	2006 World Cup Prelim

	Date	Kick-off	Match	Forecast	Venue
4.	Sun 25 June	21:00	Portugal vs. Netherlands	2:1 aet	Nuremberg

Previous games

30.06.04	Portugal vs. Netherlands	2:1 (1:0)	UEFA Euro 2004
30.04.04	Netherlands vs. Portugal	1:1 (1:0)	Friendly 2003
28.03.01	Portugal vs. Netherlands	2:2 (0:1)	2002 World Cup Prelim
11.10.00	Netherlands vs. Portugal	0:2 (0:2)	2002 World Cup Prelim

	Date	Kick-off	Match	Forecast	Venue
5.	Mon 26 June	17:00	Czech Republic vs. Australia	2:0	Kaiserslautern

Previous games

29.03.00	Czech Republic vs. Australia	3:1 (1:0)	Friendly 2000

In 2000, Iran beat Guam 19:0. Iran's population is similar to Turkey's. Guam's to that of Norwich.

Football Freaking Forecasts for the 2006 World Cup – *continued*

Second Round – *continued*

	Date	Kick-off	Match	Forecast	Venue
6.	Mon 26 June	21:00	France vs. Spain	2:1	Cologne

Previous games

28.03.01	Spain vs. France	2:1 (1:0)	Friendly 2001
25.06.00	Spain vs. France	1:2 (1:2)	UEFA Euro 2000
28.01.98	France vs. Spain	1:0 (1:0)	Friendly 1998

	Date	Kick-off	Match	Forecast	Venue
7.	Tue 27 June	17:00	Brazil vs. Ghana	3:2	Dortmund

Previous games (10 years ago)

27.03.96	Brazil vs. Ghana	8:2 (2:0)	Friendly 1996

	Date	Kick-off	Match	Forecast	Venue
8.	Tue 27 June	21:00	Tunisia vs. South Korea	1:2 aet	Hanover

Previous games

13.03.02	Tunisia vs. South Korea	0:0	Friendly 2002

Spain's best ever finish was 4th in the 1950 World Cup. Even at home, in 1982, they went out in the second round.

Football Freaking Forecasts for the 2006 World Cup – *continued*

Quarter-Finals

	Date	Kick-off	Match	Forecast	Venue
1.	Fri 30 June	17:00	Germany vs. Argentina	2:3 aet	Berlin

Summary of previous clashes
Previous games	10
Wins by Germany	3
Wins by Argentina	4
Draws	3

	Date	Kick-off	Match	Forecast	Venue
2.	Fri 30 June	21:00	Czech Republic vs. France	5:4 pso	Hamburg

Summary of previous clashes
Previous games	8
Wins by France	3
Wins by Czech Republic	1
Draws	4

	Date	Kick-off	Match	Forecast	Venue
3.	Sat 1 July	21:00	Brazil vs. South Korea	3:2 aet	Frankfurt

Summary of previous clashes
Previous games	4
Wins by Brazil	3
Wins by South Korea	1
Draws	0

	Date	Kick-off	Match	Forecast	Venue
4.	Sat 1 July	17:00	England vs. Portugal	2:1	Gelsenkirchen

Summary of previous clashes
Previous games	10
Wins by England	3
Wins by Portugal	2
Draws	5

Beating North Korea 5:3 in 1966 made Portugal the only team to ever dismiss them from a World Cup finals.

Football Freaking Forecasts for the 2006 World Cup – *continued*

Semi-Finals

	Date	Kick-off	Match	Forecast	Venue
1.	Tue 4 July	21:00	Argentina vs. Czech Republic	1:0 aet	Dortmund

Summary of previous clashes (against Czechoslovakia)

Previous games	1 (In 1958!)
Wins by Czechoslovakia	1
Wins by Argentina	0
Draws	0

Aggregate goals scored by Czechoslovakia	6
Aggregate goals scored by Argentina	1

	Date	Kick-off	Match	Forecast	Venue
2.	Wed 5 July	21:00	England vs. Brazil	0:2	Munich

Summary of previous clashes

Previous games	11
Wins by England	1
Wins by Brazil	5
Draws	5

Aggregate goals scored by England	8
Aggregate goals scored by Brazil	14

The Czech Republic debuted at the 1996 European Cup and were immediately runners-up. Scary or what?

Football Freaking Forecasts for the 2006 World Cup – *continued*

3rd-Place Play-Off

Date	Kick-off	Match	Forecast	Venue
Sat 8 July	21:00	England vs. Czech Republic	2:1 aet	Stuttgart

Summary of previous clashes (including with pre-divorce Czechoslovakia)

Previous games	5
Wins by England	4
Wins by Czech Republic	0
Draws	1

Previous games

18.11.98	England vs. Czech Republic	2:0 (2:0)	Friendly 1998

The Czech Republic may in fact win this game just to be awkward: commiserations to broken-hearted England fans everywhere; condolences to relatives of the 23 England fans whose hearts will fail altogether (see p78).

In the 3rd place play-off at the 2004 Olympics, Italy beat Iraq 1:0. Maybe the Iraqi team was distracted …

Football Freaking Forecasts for the 2006 World Cup – *continued*

Final

Date	Kick-off	Match	Forecast	Venue
Sun 9 July	20:00	Brazil vs. Argentina	2:1	Berlin

Summary of previous clashes

Previous games	26
Wins by Brazil	11
Wins by Argentina	6
Draws	9
Aggregate goals scored by Brazil	43
Aggregate goals scored by Argentina	32

Previous games

29.06.05	Brazil vs. Argentina	4:1 (2:0)	Confederations Cup
08.06.05	Argentina vs. Brazil	3:1 (3:0)	2006 World Cup Prelim
25.07.04	Argentina vs. Brazil	2:4 pso	Copa America 2004
02.06.04	Brazil vs. Argentina	3:1 (1:0)	2006 World Cup Prelim

In 2000, an internet poll found about 3 times as many fans consider Maradona the player of the 20th century as opposed to Pelé. For which player do you think England fans would have voted?

Brazil first played Argentina in 1914.

What Every Man Wants:
The Ultimate Trophy Book

Andrew Mann

Introduced by
Frankie Dettori

The Ryder Cup, the
Ashes, the FA Cup,
the Claret Jug, the
Webb Ellis, the Green
Jacket, the Stanley,
the Americas: men
have always loved
their trophies.

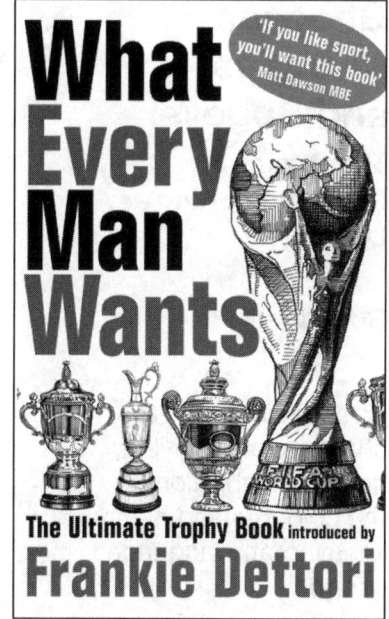

Whatever their game of
choice, winning its ultimate prize is something nearly every
man has dreamed about. Thanks to this brilliant guide to the
most celebrated trophies in the world, he can now get close
enough to almost taste the glory.

What Every Man Wants unearths the essentials on every
revered tournament prize that has ever been fought over in
modern times, including:

- the reasons behind the bizarre codes of sporting conduct
  linked to each trophy
- who you're up against if you want to get involved
- tips on how to collect the silverware
- what can't be found in any rulebook and why it's not just
  the 'taking part' that counts.

Hardback £9.99

ISBN 10: 1 84046 775 4   ISBN 13: 978 1840467 75 8

Googlies, Nutmegs and Bogeys:

The Origins of Peculiar Sporting Lingo

Bob Wilson

Bob Wilson offers a champagne-spraying, riotous celebration of the colourful and highly idiosyncratic language of sport.

Googlies, Nutmegs & Bogeys

The Origins of Peculiar Sporting Lingo

BOB WILSON

Have you ever flashed at a googly in the corridor of uncertainty while on a sticky dog? Maybe you've seen someone hit a gutty out of the screws to grab a birdie at Amen Corner?

The world of sport has its own language, rich in strange words and phrases whose origins often stretch back centuries. *Googlies, Nutmegs and Bogeys* is an illustrated lexicon – unravelling the true meanings, heritage and evolution of sporting terms – that makes the perfect companion guide to the glorious abusrdities of sporting vocabulary that continue to enliven the English language today.

Hardback £9.99

ISBN 10: 1 84046 774 6   ISBN 13: 978 1840467 74 1

101 Facts You Should Know About Food

John Farndon

Attention-grabbing facts and punchy popular analysis of the things you really should know about the food you eat.

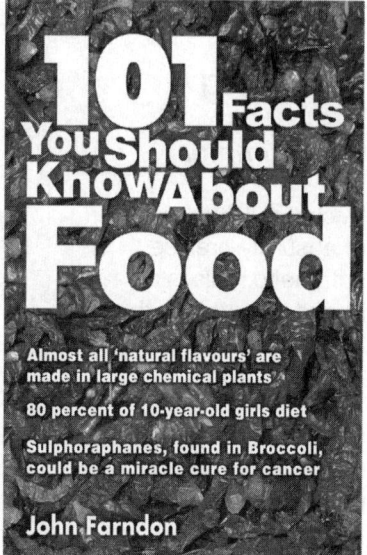

- The largest modern fishing trawler drags a net twice the volume of the Millennium Dome
- A jar of instant coffee costs 7,000 per cent more than the farmer receives for it
- High-yielding turkeys have such large breasts they cannot have sex
- A single fast food meal causes similar changes in brain chemistry to class A drugs
- The biggest beneficiaries of the EU's farm subsidies are not farmers but food manufacturers

From the extraordinary distance most of our food travels to reach our tables to the remarkable benefits of eating tomatoes, John Farndon shows the amazing, often shocking, truth behind the food we eat. Covering everything from the big businesses that control food production around the world to the dangers of food dyes, this book reveals the complex facts behind the simplest of meals.

Find out just what GM food is and why you may eat it unknowingly, how food gets its flavour, how some foods are not quite as nutritious as they should be, how bringing exotic foods to your table may literally be costing the Earth, and much more.

This is an essential guide to the facts behind food, the one vital thing in your life besides air and water – and the world's biggest business.

Paperback £6.99

ISBN 10: 1 84046 767 3   ISBN 13: 978 1840467 67 3

Number Freaking

Gary Rimmer

'A cheerful little mix of absurdly precise arithmetic. This is a book for nutters with calculators and a lot of fun.' *Guardian*

'Gary Rimmer is the Sam Spade of number puzzles, an ambassador for freaking figures, a one-man waterfall of bizarre maths facts.' *Sunday Telegraph*

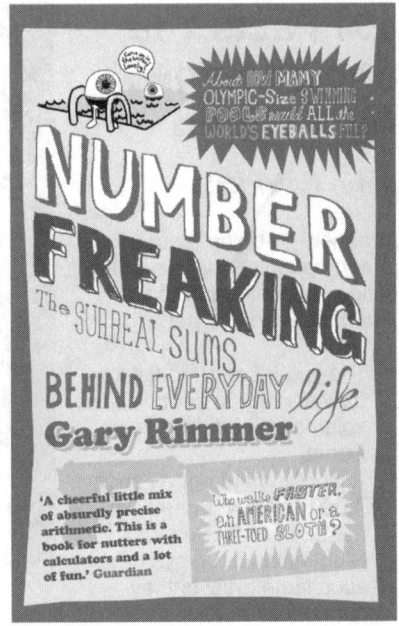

From sex and celebrity to science and sport – *Number Freaking* provides the answers to every question you never needed to ask.

- When will America collide with Japan?
- Why did Elvis really die?
- What's a decent girlfriend worth?
- Which is more crowded: Jakarta, Ikea or Hell?
- How many people on Earth are drunk right now?

Discover for yourself how far you walk in a lifetime, how many people have ever lived and how to cure world debt in the ultimate guide to modern life …

Paperback £7.99

ISBN 10: 1 84046 751 7   ISBN 13: 978 1840467 51 2